Lecture Notes in Computer Science 14205

Founding Editors

Gerhard Goos

Juris Hartmanis

Editorial Board Members

Elisa Bertino, *Purdue University, West Lafayette, IN, USA*

Wen Gao, *Peking University, Beijing, China*

Bernhard Steffen, *TU Dortmund University, Dortmund, Germany*

Moti Yung, *Columbia University, New York, NY, USA*

The series Lecture Notes in Computer Science (LNCS), including its subseries Lecture Notes in Artificial Intelligence (LNAI) and Lecture Notes in Bioinformatics (LNBI), has established itself as a medium for the publication of new developments in computer science and information technology research, teaching, and education.

LNCS enjoys close cooperation with the computer science R & D community, the series counts many renowned academics among its volume editors and paper authors, and collaborates with prestigious societies. Its mission is to serve this international community by providing an invaluable service, mainly focused on the publication of conference and workshop proceedings and postproceedings. LNCS commenced publication in 1973.

Jun Feng · Frank Jiang · Min Luo ·
Liang-Jie Zhang

Editors

Edge Computing – EDGE 2023

7th International Conference
Held as Part of the Services Conference Federation, SCF 2023
Shenzhen, China, December 17–18, 2023
Proceedings

Springer

Editors
Jun Feng
Huazhong University of Science
and Technology
Wuhan, China

Min Luo
Georgia Institute of Technology
Atlanta, GA, USA

Frank Jiang
Deakin University
Burwood, VIC, Australia

Liang-Jie Zhang ⓘ
Shenzhen Entrepreneurship and Innovation
Federation
Shenzhen, China

ISSN 0302-9743   ISSN 1611-3349 (electronic)
Lecture Notes in Computer Science
ISBN 978-3-031-51825-6   ISBN 978-3-031-51826-3 (eBook)
https://doi.org/10.1007/978-3-031-51826-3

This Springer imprint is published by the registered company Springer Nature Switzerland AG
The registered company address is: Gewerbestrasse 11, 6330 Cham, Switzerland

Paper in this product is recyclable.

Preface

The International Conference on Edge Computing (EDGE) aimed to become a prime international forum for both researchers and industry practitioners to exchange the latest fundamental advances in the state of the art and practice of edge computing, identify emerging research topics, and define the future of edge computing.

EDGE 2023 was a member of the Services Conference Federation (SCF). SCF 2023 had the following 10 collocated service-oriented sister conferences: the 2023 International Conference on Web Services (ICWS 2023), the 2023 International Conference on Cloud Computing (CLOUD 2023), the 2023 International Conference on Services Computing (SCC 2023), the 2023 International Conference on Big Data (BigData 2023), the 2023 International Conference on AI & Mobile Services (AIMS 2023), the 2023 International Conference on Metaverse (Metaverse 2023), the 2023 International Conference on Internet of Things (ICIOT 2023), the 2023 International Conference on Cognitive Computing (ICCC 2023), the 2023 International Conference on Edge Computing (EDGE 2023), and the 2023 International Conference on Blockchain (ICBC 2023). As the founding member of SCF, the 1st International Conference on Web Services (ICWS) was held in June 2003 in Las Vegas, USA. Meanwhile, the 1st International Conference on Web Services - Europe 2003 (ICWS-Europe 2003) was held in Germany in 2003. ICWS-Europe 2003 was an extended event of the 2003 International Conference on Web Services (ICWS 2003) in Europe. In 2004, ICWS-Europe was changed to the European Conference on Web Services (ECOWS), which was held in Erfurt, Germany.

This volume presents the accepted papers for the 2023 International Conference on Edge Computing (EDGE 2023), held in Shenzhen, during December 17–18, 2023. For EDGE 2023, there were 14 submissions, we accepted 8 papers for the proceedings. Each was reviewed and selected by at least three independent members of the EDGE 2023 International Program Committee in a single-blind review process.

We are pleased to thank the authors whose submissions and participation made this conference possible. We also want to express our thanks to the Organizing Committee and Program Committee members, for their dedication in helping to organize the conference and reviewing the submissions. We look forward to your great contributions as volunteers, authors, and conference participants in the fast-growing worldwide services innovations community.

December 2023

Jun Feng
Frank Jiang
Min Luo
Liang-Jie Zhang

Organization

General Chair

Jinpeng Wei   University of North Carolina at Charlotte, USA

Program Chairs

Min Luo   Georgia Tech, USA
Frank Jiang   Deakin University, Australia
Jun Feng   Huazhong University of Science and Technology, China

Services Conference Federation (SCF 2023)

General Chairs

Ali Arsanjani   Google, USA
Wu Chou   Essenlix Corporation, USA

Coordinating Program Chair

Liang-Jie Zhang   Shenzhen Entrepreneurship & Innovation Federation, China

CFO and International Affairs Chair

Min Luo   Georgia Tech, USA

Operation Committee

Jing Zeng   China Gridcom, China
Yishuang Ning   Tsinghua University, China
Sheng He   Tsinghua University, China

Steering Committee

Calton Pu (Co-chair)	Georgia Tech, USA
Liang-Jie Zhang (Co-chair)	Shenzhen Entrepreneurship & Innovation Federation, China

ICIOT 2023 Program Committee

Xianghan Zheng	Fuzhou University, China
Le Chang	Guangdong University of Technology, China
Tao Han	New Jersey Institute of Technology, USA
Tessema Mengistu	Virginia Tech, USA
Rui André Oliveira	University of Lisbon, Portugal
Weichao Wang	University of North Carolina at Charlotte, USA
Mengjun Xie	University of Tennessee at Chattanooga, USA
Ozgur Ertug	Gazi University, Turkey
Midori Sugaya	Shibaura Institute of Technology, Japan
Javid Taheri	Karlstad University, Sweden
Hung-Yu Wei	National Taiwan University, China
Fangming Liu	Huazhong University of Science and Technology, China
Ahmed El Oualkadi	LabTIC Abdelmalek Essaadi University, Morocco

Conference Sponsor – Services Society

The Services Society (S2) is a non-profit professional organization that has been created to promote worldwide research and technical collaboration in services innovations among academia and industrial professionals. Its members are volunteers from industry and academia with common interests. S2 is registered in the USA as a "501(c) organization", which means that it is an American tax-exempt nonprofit organization. S2 collaborates with other professional organizations to sponsor or co-sponsor conferences and to promote an effective services curriculum in colleges and universities. S2 initiates and promotes a "Services University" program worldwide to bridge the gap between industrial needs and university instruction.

The services sector accounted for 79.5% of the GDP of the USA in 2016. The Services Society has formed 5 Special Interest Groups (SIGs) to support technology- and domain-specific professional activities.

- Special Interest Group on Services Computing (SIG-SC)
- Special Interest Group on Big Data (SIG-BD)
- Special Interest Group on Cloud Computing (SIG-CLOUD)
- Special Interest Group on Artificial Intelligence (SIG-AI)
- Special Interest Group on Metaverse (SIG-Metaverse)

About the Services Conference Federation (SCF)

As the founding member of the Services Conference Federation (SCF), the first **International Conference on Web Services (ICWS)** was held in June 2003 in Las Vegas, USA. Meanwhile, the 1st International Conference on Web Services - Europe 2003 (ICWS-Europe 2003) was held in Germany in October 2003. ICWS-Europe 2003 was an extended event of the 2003 International Conference on Web Services (ICWS 2003) in Europe. In 2004, ICWS-Europe was changed to the European Conference on Web Services (ECOWS), which was held in Erfurt, Germany. Sponsored by the Services Society, SCF 2018 and SCF 2019 were held successfully in Seattle and San Diego, USA. SCF 2020 and SCF 2021 were held successfully online and in Shenzhen, China. SCF 2022 was held successfully in Hawaii, USA. To celebrate its 21st birthday, SCF 2023 phase-I was held on September 23–26, 2023, in Honolulu, Hawaii, USA and SCF 2023 phase-II was on December 17–18, 2023, in Shenzhen, Guangdong, China. SCF 2023 phase-II was hosted by the Services Society and the Shenzhen Entrepreneurship & Innovation Federation (SEIF).

In the past 20 years, the ICWS community has been expanded from Web engineering innovations to scientific research for the whole services industry. The service delivery platforms have been expanded to mobile platforms, Internet of Things, cloud computing, and edge computing. The services ecosystem has gradually been enabled, value added, and intelligence embedded through enabling technologies such as big data, artificial intelligence, and cognitive computing. In the coming years, all transactions with multiple parties involved will be transformed to blockchain.

Based on technology trends and best practices in the field, the Services Conference Federation (SCF) will continue serving as the conference umbrella's code name for all services-related conferences. SCF 2023 defined the future of New ABCDE (AI, Blockchain, Cloud, Big Data & IOT) and we entered the 5G for Services Era. The theme of SCF 2023 was the Metaverse Era. We are very proud to announce that SCF 2023's 10 co-located theme topic conferences all centered around "services", while each focused on exploring different themes (web-based services, cloud-based services, Big Data-based services, services innovation lifecycle, AI-driven ubiquitous services, blockchain-driven trust service-ecosystems, industry-specific services and applications, and emerging service-oriented technologies).

- Bigger Platform: The 10 collocated conferences (SCF 2023) were sponsored by the Services Society, which is the world-leading not-for-profit organization (501 c(3)) dedicated to the service of more than 30,000 worldwide Services Computing researchers and practitioners. A bigger platform means bigger opportunities for all volunteers, authors, and participants. Meanwhile, Springer provided sponsorship to best paper awards and other professional activities. All the 10 conference proceedings of SCF 2023 will be published by Springer and indexed in ISI Conference Proceedings Citation Index (included in Web of Science), Engineering Index EI (Compendex

and Inspec databases), DBLP, Google Scholar, IO-Port, MathSciNet, Scopus, and ZBlMath.
- Brighter Future: While celebrating the 2023 version of ICWS, SCF 2023 highlighted the 2nd International Conference on Metaverse (METAVERSE 2023), which covered immersive services for all vertical industries and area solutions. Its focus was on industry-specific services for digital transformation. This will lead our community members to create their own brighter futures.
- Better Model: SCF 2023 will continue to leverage the invented Conference Blockchain Model (CBM) to innovate the organizing practices for all 10 theme conferences. Senior researchers in the field were welcome to submit proposals to serve as CBM Ambassadors for individual conferences to start better interactions during their leadership roles in organizing future SCF conferences.

Contents

Research and Application of Low Voltage Distributed Power Supply Control System

Shida She[1], Tongwei Yu[1], Junxiong Ge[2], Haimin Hong[2], Zhenhong Yan[1], Tong Wang[1], Wuyang Zhang[1], and Mingfeng Shi[2(✉)]

[1] Electric Power Research Institute of State Grid Liaoning Electric Power Co., Ltd., Shenyang 110006, China
[2] China Gridcom Co., Ltd., Shenzhen 518109, China
shimingfeng@sgchip.sgcc.com.cn

Abstract. With the launch of the National Energy Administration's rooftop photovoltaic pilot construction in all counties and cities, power companies in various provinces and cities of the State Grid are facing severe safety management challenges. For example, distributed power sources such as photovoltaic and wind power are affected by natural weather, and their output is intermittent and difficult to control. Large-scale integration into the power system will have an impact on the power system, making it unable to operate normally, and even leading to power system collapse and damage to power equipment. Therefore, it is necessary to form a low-cost solution that meets the basic requirements of stable and safe operation of the power grid. In this paper, we propose a regulation scheme of low-voltage distributed generation, which uses the edge computing capability deployed in the distribution transformer fusion terminal, and the communication capability of power line carrier and the intelligent circuit breaker integrated with function fusion to realize the observation and control of distributed energy and electrical equipment. The proposed scheme has been piloted and verified in two typical power distribution areas in Shenyang, and the pilot application has achieved the expected goals.

Keywords: Photovoltaic · Distributed Generation · Regulation · Power Line Carrier · Fusion Terminal · Intelligent Circuit Breaker

1 Introduction

Driven by the carbon peak and carbon neutrality goals, renewable energy such as photovoltaic power generation will become increasingly widespread. The application of distributed power sources such as photovoltaic power generation in low-voltage distribution networks can not only reduce carbon emissions and pollutants, but also effectively solve the problem of "low voltage" in rural power grids [1, 16], so it can meet human needs of energy and help address the issues of energy shortages. The distributed photovoltaic power supply connected to the distribution network is divided into three states: normal, early warning, and emergency [2]. Under normal operating conditions, it

J. Feng et al. (Eds.): EDGE 2023, LNCS 14205, pp. 1–13, 2024.
https://doi.org/10.1007/978-3-031-51826-3_1

achieves maximum absorption of photovoltaic power supply; In the early warning state, while maximizing the active output of the photovoltaic power supply, it eliminates the hidden dangers of safe operation of the distribution network; In an emergency state, it quickly adjusts the voltage of the distribution network to reach a safe operating state [3, 4].

At present, the major researches on photovoltaic distributed power are divided into two-fold: 1) one is to study the distribution network issues of photovoltaic power generation [12, 14–19]; 2) another is to study the relay protection problem of photovoltaic power generation[22–25]. The above researches mainly verify the feasibility and reliability of distributed power generation in practical applications through modeling and simulation, but there are no practical applications.

In the practical applications of renewable energy such as photovoltaic power generation, not only the feasibility and reliability of photovoltaic power generation connected to the power grid should be considered, but also their practicality and economy.

Currently, there is no regulating approaches to address the integration of renewable energy sources such as photovoltaic power generation into the power grid. Therefore, monitoring rooftop photovoltaics in rural and suburban areas will pose challenges to the operation and maintenance safety and flow control of the regional power grid [19]. Various departments of the power grid have put forward requirements for their measurement, power quality, anti islanding protection, and emergency regulation. Due to its wide geographical distribution, it brings high cost pressure to the implementation of secondary systems.

In order to counter these challenges and to implement the control requirements of State Grid Corporation of China for flexible resources such as low-voltage distributed photovoltaics, standardizing the grid connection technology scheme of low-voltage distributed power sources, and ensuring the safe operation of the power grid, this paper proposes an economical and practical low-voltage distributed power supply control system solution, which integrates various links such as procurement, transmission, storage, and use, to achieve the observability, measurability, and controllability of distributed power sources [5–7]. It provide a practical foundation for the application of microgrids such as photovoltaic power generation in ordinary households [11].

2   The Proposed Scheme

The low-voltage distributed power supply regulation scheme proposed in this article consists of a distribution automation master station, an intelligent fusion terminal, a photovoltaic intelligent circuit breaker, and a photovoltaic inverter. The system architecture is shown in Fig. 1.

The intelligent fusion terminal in the substation area communicates with the photovoltaic intelligent circuit breaker on HPLC communication channels. The data of photovoltaic intelligent circuit breaker is encrypted through IEC101 protocol after edge computing, then it is sent to the distribution automation master station. The information, which is sent to the master station, includes remote sensing data, such as photovoltaic quantity, photovoltaic capacity, photovoltaic power generation power, as well as remote signaling data, such as power off events, abnormal events of time synchronization, switch

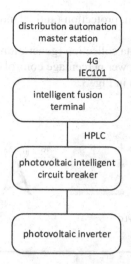

Fig. 1. The System Architecture

position status, etc. The functional architecture of the Proposed Scheme is shown in Fig. 2.

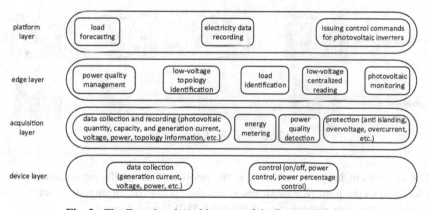

Fig. 2. The Functional Architecture of the Proposed Scheme

The functional architecture is divided into four layers: platform layer, edge layer, acquisition layer, and device layer.

The platform layer includes load forecasting, electricity data recording, and issuing control commands for photovoltaic inverters;

The edge layer includes: power quality management, low-voltage topology identification, load identification, low-voltage centralized reading, photovoltaic monitoring, etc.;

The collection layer includes: data collection and recording (photovoltaic quantity, capacity, and generation current, voltage, power, topology information, etc.), energy metering, power quality detection, protection (anti islanding, overvoltage, overcurrent, etc.);

The device layer includes: data collection (generation current, voltage, power, etc.), control (on/off, power control, power percentage control).

The site layout plan is shown in Fig. 3.

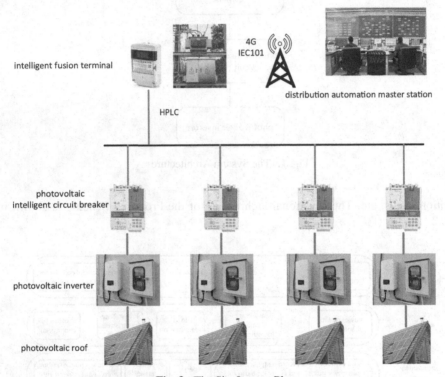

Fig. 3. The Site Layout Plan

The equipment layout is as follows: the photovoltaic intelligent circuit breaker is installed next to the photovoltaic inverter, and the substation intelligent fusion terminal is installed on the low-voltage side of the 10kV/0.4kV transformer.

The Theoretical and Practical Basis for the plan:

(1) The Power Line Carrier is a communication method that uses power cables as a medium for information or data transmission. The basic principle of its communication is: the process of sending data involves the signal being encoded, analog-to-digital converted, filtered, and amplified, then coupled to the power line through a coupling unit for transmission. The process of receiving data is to separate the signal on the power line through a coupling unit, and obtain the data at the sending end through analog-to-digital conversion, filtering, and decoding.

The practical basis for Power Line Carrier is that in June 2017, State Grid Corporation of China issued the "Q/GDW11612 Technical Specification for Low Voltage High Speed

Carrier Communication Interconnection and Interoperability". In 2019, China Southern Power Grid organized relevant manufacturers to prepare the "Technical Requirements for Broadband Carrier Communication of Power Lines in Measurement Automation Systems". The relevant technical specifications issued by State Grid and China Southern Power Grid Corporation have clearly defined the requirements for the physical layer, data link layer, and the application layer of Power Line Carrier. Medium Voltage Power Line Carrier is a limited private network communication method that does not require line investment, and it can be applied to remote communication from acquisition terminals or concentrators to substations. The Medium Voltage Power Line Carrier can be used to improve the success rate of electricity information collection, especially when it is applied to data collection for users in mountainous areas with weak and unstable signals.

(2) The practical basis for the integrated fusion terminal system is that the intelligent terminal in the substation area is based on specifications, such as "Technical Specification for Intelligent Integrated Terminals in the Substation Area", "Interface Protocol for Functional Modules of Intelligent Integrated Terminals in the Substation Area", "Technical Specification for Functional Modules of Intelligent Integrated Terminals in the Substation Area", "Development Specification for Micro Applications of Integrated Terminals in the Substation Area", and "Type Specification for Functional Modules of Intelligent Integrated Terminals in the Substation Area", which meet national standards Regulations and the actual needs of the majority of power users.

The hardware consists of a main control board and a power board, which is based on a gallium nitride (GaN) power module for power conversion module and connected to a functional module through a reserved module interface to achieve functional integration.

In terms of software, the application software framework is designed based on object-oriented methods following the principles of "hardware platformization and software APPization". The Linux kernel is transplanted into domestic chip hardware as an open platform. The application software is designed as APP software running within a unified operating system.

The integration fusion terminal integrates and optimizes the operation monitoring and measurement equipment in the distribution station area, which can replace the original distribution transformer monitoring and measurement terminal and power consumption data information collection concentrator in the distribution station area. With implementing all the functions of the two devices, we can configure corresponding extension modules and APP according to the actual application scenarios of the terminal, such as power quality management, topology identification of low-voltage, load identification, etc.

(3) State Grid Jiangsu Electric Power Co., Ltd. Has revised the original technical specifications for low voltage molded case circuit breakers and added requirements for communication protocols, including: "Communication Protocol for Low Voltage

Molded Case Circuit Breakers with Leakage Protection Function", "Communication Protocol for Low Voltage Molded Case Circuit Breakers with No Leakage Protection Function", "Installation and Operation of Residual Current Action Protection Devices in GB 13955" GB 50150 Electrical Equipment Installation Engineering Electrical Equipment Handover Test Standard. The intelligent circuit breaker utilizes intelligent low-voltage switches to achieve real-time monitoring of low-voltage switch operating conditions and active reporting of low-voltage power outage events, achieving panoramic perception of the operating situation in the low-voltage substation area, achieving "physical examination" operation and maintenance of low-voltage power grids and "diagnostic" emergency repair of equipment faults.

The advantages of this solution are:

(1) Using 4G and HPLC to transmit data, the observability and testability of power data are improved, construction wiring is reduced, and installation costs are reduced;
(2) Using intelligent circuit breakers with multiple functions, such as measurement and protection, the scope of fault isolation can be reduced, fault points can be quickly located, the cause of power outages can be identified, troubleshooting time can be reduced, operation and maintenance costs can be reduced, and the controllability of power sources can be improved, thereby improving the stability and safety of power system operation;
(3) Edge computing is done in the fusion terminal. Through the collected basic data, such as distribution network operation status, equipment status, environmental status and other auxiliary information, the decision command or local control can be quickly executed to shorten the power control time.

The difficulty of this solution lies in:

(1) Data is communicated on power line carrier channel between multiple terminals under centralized meter reading system, i.e. information is communicated between any two nodes;
(2) The competition between centralized acquisition systems and other systems in the integration terminal for carrier communication channels;
(3) Intelligent circuit breakers integrate energy metering, anti islanding protection, collaboration with fusion terminals, and collaboration with photovoltaic inverters.

3   The Pilot Test

The purpose of this pilot test is to verify the feasibility and reliability of the power regulation scheme in rooftop photovoltaic power plants. Technical design indicators are: active power measurement error limit: $\pm$ 0.5%, whether the protection action is accurate, and verify the observability, measurability, and controllability of this scheme for distributed power sources.

The experimental content is to conduct on-site testing at the location of the intelligent fusion terminal in the substation area, and to test the communication between the fusion terminal and the circuit breaker using an applicable mobile phone operation and maintenance app. In the low-voltage measurement and control unit, we check the number, power type, logical address of the photovoltaic intelligent circuit breaker, and the communication connection. We test the collection of photovoltaic data, grid connection protection function, anti islanding protection function, and stability.

3.1   Tests and the Result Analysis

The Photovoltaic Data Collection. We change the capacity value of the photovoltaic system at the position of the photovoltaic intelligent circuit breaker, use the mobile operation and maintenance app to connect to the intelligent integration terminal in the substation area through Bluetooth, continuously refresh the single circuit breaker and the aggregated total photovoltaic power generation data, and verify the real-time and accuracy of the photovoltaic power generation data (Figs. 4 and 5).

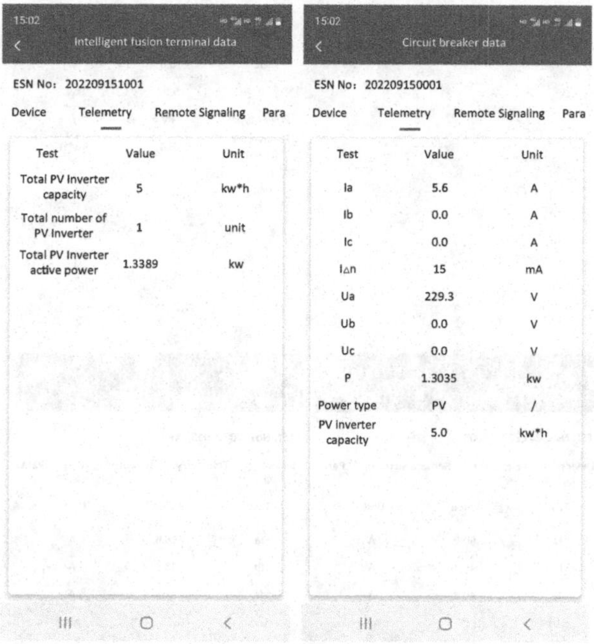

Fig. 4. The Photovoltaic Data Collection of Pilot 1

Table 1 shows the photovoltaic power generation data of two stations monitored by the distribution automation main station during the testing period on November 4, 2022.

According to the data in the table, the maximum error between the power generation data and the lighting is less than 0.5%, and the remaining data errors are consistent with the data, which meets the design technical indicators and the accuracy requirements of the control system for the collected data.

The Test of The Functions of Photovoltaic Grid Connection Protection. We test photovoltaic grid connection protection function at the position of the photovoltaic intelligent circuit breaker. The incoming end of the photovoltaic intelligent circuit breaker is connected to the low-voltage power grid, and the outgoing end is connected to the photovoltaic inverter. The circuit breaker is in an open state, and normal voltage is applied

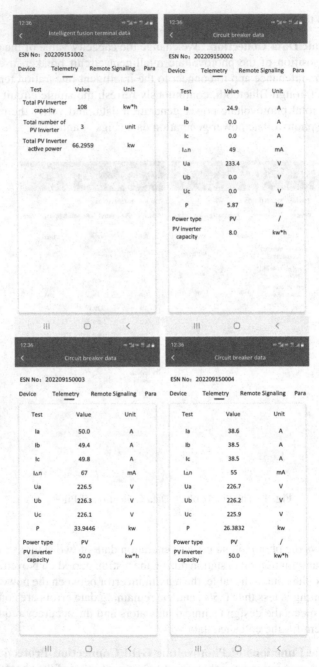

Fig. 5. The Photovoltaic Data Collection of Pilot 2

Table 1. The data statistical analysis

Time	Pilot 1 Number of Photovoltaic inverters: 1 Photovoltaic power capacity:5kW			Pilot 2 Number of Photovoltaic inverters: 3 Photovoltaic capacity: 108kW		
	Value /kW	Photovoltaic capacity /kW	Error /%	Value /kW	Photovoltaic capacity /kW	Error /%
November 4th 6:02	0	0	/	0	0	/
November 4th 7:03	0.0443	0.0442	0.2262	12.3802	12.3512	0.2348
November 4th 8:01	1.0103	1.0106	-0.0297	20.2267	20.1929	0.1674
November 4th 9:05	1.4721	1.4719	0.0136	46.4323	46.3562	0.1642
November 4th 10:03	1.6536	1.6502	0.2060	53.5133	53.4227	0.1696
November 4th 11:02	1.8932	1.8891	0.2170	60.3596	60.2576	0.1693
November 4th 12:01	1.9501	1.9462	0.2004	62.2265	62.1221	0.1681
November 4th 13:03	1.9223	1.9203	0.1042	60.5347	60.4347	0.1655
November 4th 14:02	1.6198	1.6165	0.2041	51.7212	51.6359	0.1652
November 4th 15:05	1.3476	1.3455	0.1561	44.9449	44.8712	0.1642
November 4th 16:01	1.0307	1.0292	0.1457	20.3957	20.3602	0.1744
November 4th 17:02	0.0223	0.0222	0.4505	0.5932	0.5911	0.3553

to the incoming and outgoing ends of the circuit breaker. The circuit breaker should prohibit the operation of the closing motor. When normal voltage and frequency are applied to the incoming end of the circuit breaker, where is no voltage at the outgoing end, the circuit breaker should be able to close the circuit breaker by driving the motor.

The photovoltaic intelligent circuit breakers in both stations can correctly connect to the grid based on the voltage and frequency of the incoming and outgoing terminals. Repeat the test 10 times and all actions are correct.

The Test of The Function of Anti Islanding Protection. We test anti islanding protection function at the location of the photovoltaic intelligent circuit breaker. We open the isolation switch at the incoming end of the photovoltaic intelligent circuit breaker and simulate a low-voltage power grid outage to verify whether the circuit breaker operates correctly within 2 s.

The photovoltaic intelligent circuit breakers in the two substations can accurately identify the characteristics of island operating conditions after a low-voltage power grid outage, and correctly trip within 2 s. Repeat the test 10 times and all actions are correct.

The Test of Stability. We conduct on-site testing at the location of the intelligent fusion terminal in the substation area, allowing the low-voltage distributed power control system to operate for a long time. We monitor the online status and system stability of the intelligent fusion terminal on main station of distribution network automation.

The fusion terminals of the two stations can correctly collect and transmit photovoltaic data to the distribution automation main station at the same time. During the testing period, the accuracy rate of collected data reached over 99.5%.

Through the collection and testing of photovoltaic data, it can be seen that this scheme is observable and testable for distributed power source data. Through testing the photovoltaic grid connection protection and anti islanding protection, it can be seen that this scheme is controllable for distributed power source data. Through stability testing, it can be seen that this scheme meets the basic requirements for stability and safety of power system operation. When distributed power is connected to the grid, the observability, testability, and controllability of low-voltage distributed power regulation system solutions can reduce the difficulty of power load prediction in distribution stations, increase the certainty of distribution network planning, and enhance the adaptability of distribution network planning.

3.2   The Problems and Analysis of the Test

(1) The intelligent integration fusion terminal in pilot 1 has the problem of being unable to form a network with photovoltaic intelligent circuit breakers through HPLC.

Problem analysis. The distance between the power line is too far, so it results in the inability to form a network between the terminal and the circuit breaker through HPLC. We conduct power line survey. It was found that the distance between the intelligent fusion terminal and the photovoltaic circuit breaker in pilot area 1 exceeded 500 m. Before the pilot, only the position distance between the two terminals was visually measured. After visual inspection, the distance did not exceed 150 m, but the power line distance was ignored.

Solution. We put an HPLC repeater device in the middle of the line between the substation intelligent fusion terminal and the photovoltaic intelligent circuit breaker to repeat and amplify the signal, which can achieve rapid networking between the substation intelligent fusion terminal and the photovoltaic circuit breaker.

(2) There is a problem in pilot 2 one photovoltaic intelligent circuit breaker takes a long time to integrate with the intelligent terminal network in the substation area.

Problem analysis. It takes a long time for one photovoltaic circuit breaker to form a network with the intelligent fusion terminal in the substation area. Upon checking with the controller, it was found that the network level is relatively low, to indicate low signal quality and affect the HPLC network.

Solution. We optimize the signal spectrum and error vector amplitude of the CCO and STA of the intelligent fusion terminal and circuit breaker in the substation area through software. The reliability of data transmission can be improved, and interference with other terminals can be reduced. We view through the controller. The network level can be increased by 2 levels, enabling rapid networking.

(3) There is a problem data acquisition is lossed at the intelligent fusion terminal in pilot 2.

Problem analysis. During the data collection of circuit breakers at the fusion terminal, it was found that data was lossed. The data is affected the judgment of the main station on the distributed photovoltaic power generation situation.

Solution. We optimize the data collection items and methods of the intelligent integration terminal in the substation area for circuit breakers, focusing on collecting data, such as distributed energy type, photovoltaic capacity, power generation, voltage and current of circuit breakers, leakage current, and switch opening times. We add a fault tolerance mechanism, such as judging the collected data and discovering data loss. Multiple data collection can be carried out to effectively solve the problem of data loss.

4 Conclusions

Driven by the carbon peak and carbon neutrality goals, renewable energy will be widely used in the field of power generation. Distributed power generation as the main application solution needs to be considered from stability, reliability, economy, practicality, and other aspects in practical engineering. After this experiment, from several aspects such as equipment installation, debugging, reliability, and stability, the photovoltaic distributed power supply regulation test is summarized as follows:

(1) During the pilot period, the communication between the distribution automation main station, substation integration terminal, and photovoltaic intelligent circuit breaker was stable, and abnormal data transmission situations did not happened. It was able to accurately report the distributed photovoltaic power generation situation to the main station.
(2) The photovoltaic intelligent circuit breaker works normally and meets the pre-set design indicators for photovoltaic grid connection protection, anti islanding protection, energy metering, residual current protection, etc.

Based on the various test results of this pilot project, it is fully demonstrated that the low-voltage distributed power supply control system collects accurate data, has stable protection functions, meets the design indicators of the scheme, and meets the requirements of observability, measurability, and controllability for distributed power supply. This provides a practical foundation for the application of microgrids.

References

1. Li, Y., Ji, J.: Research on the problem of low voltage in low voltage network based on access to distributed power. Agricul. Sci. Technol. Equipment (7), 40–42 (2016)
2. Meng, X., Pu, Z., Xie, D., Shi, M.: Distributed generation optimal placing approach in rural power network. J. Agricul. Eng. **26**(8), 243–247 (2010)
3. Liu, C., Wang, H., Wen, J., Xian, Z., Deng, Y.: Research on grid-connected consumption control of distributed photovoltaic power generation based on carbon neutrality target. Indus. Heating **52**(1), 49–53 (2023)
4. Yuan, F., Zhao, J., Guo, B., Tian, Y., Wang, X., Wang, Y.: Research on coordinated control strategy of distributed photovoltaic generation and distribution network. Elect. Measurem. Instrum. **57**(24), 116–124 (2020)
5. Zhu, L., Fu, D., Zhai, J., Chen, D.: Analysis of influence of distributed photovoltaic generation upon node voltage of the distribution network. Elect. Autom. **40**(6), 74–77 (2018)
6. Zhong, M., Hu, D., Long, J., Zhou, Z.: Application and prospect of low voltage distributed power supply control and acquisition device achievements. Power Equipm. Manag. **86**(20), 135–137 (2022)
7. Zheng, C., Zhu, G., Lan, J., Li, S.: Research on the effect of inverter interfaced distributed generation on voltage-time feeder automation. Power Syst. Prot. Control **48**(1), 112–116 (2020)
8. Zhang, M., Piao, Z.: Research of Distribution network peak shaving for distributed grid-connected pv system with energy storage device. Elect. Eng. **206**(12), 11–14, 19 (2016)
9. Yang, Q., Liu, J., Jiang, W.: Peak Regulation strategy of power system considering the inter-action of source-network-load-storage under different penetration rate of PV. Electric Power Const. **42**(9), 74–84 (2021)
10. Han, X., Liu, W., Pan, Q., Shen, Z., Li, Y.: Peak shaving control model of power load participation system considering day-ahead spot market risk. Power Syst. Protect. Control **50**(17), 55–67 (2022)
11. Zhu, H., Li, Y., Li, F., Sun, H., Zhang, H., Chen, J.: Distributed collaborative expansion planning method for electricity-gas distribution network based on analytical target cascading. Smart Power **49**(12), 72–79 (2021)
12. Zhang, K., Wang, G., Geng, X., Jia, Z., Li, X., Shen, Y.: Distributed cooperative control strategy for grid-connected power in ADN with high proportion of PV-ESS units. J. Electric Power Sci. Technol. **37**(2), 147–155 (2022)
13. Li, Y., Lü, N., Liu, X., Hu, J., Xu, Y.: Output evaluation method of distributed photovoltaic cluster considering renewable energy accommodation and power loss of network. Electric Power Const. **43**(10), 136–146 (2022)
14. Liu, J., Lin, T., Zhao, J., Wang, P., Su, B., Fan, X.: Specific planning of distribution automation systems based on the requirement of service reliability. Power Syst. Protect. Control **413**(11), 52–60 (2014)
15. Yang, Y., Huo, L., Tang, C., Shi, N., Li, H.: Collaborative planning method for distributed power and distribution automation terminal. China Sci. Technol. Papers **16**(11), 1263–1270 (2021)
16. Yang, S., Cheng, M.: Study on DG optimal distribution in distribution network. Smart Power **40**(10), 23–26 (2012)
17. Zhu, C., Li, C., Song, L., Wu, Q., Liu, B.: Distribution automation system planning considering power grid expansion. J. Electric Power Sci. Technol. **139**(6), 11–19 (2021)
18. Huang, H., Gao, S., Zhu, L., Jiang, N., Yang, K.: Research on adaptive optimization method for distribution automation of grid structure. Electr. Design Eng. **28**(11), 84–87 (2020)

19. Weng, X., Chen, Y., Huang, H., Xu, N., Wu, Z.: Planning method of distribution network feeder automation in mountain area considering distributed generation. Mech. Elect. Eng. Technol. **325**(4), 178–182 (2019)
20. Li, Y., Zhang, Z., Luo, R., Xue, J., Xin, C., Xu, L.: Integrated energy system planning method combined with microgrid operation mode. Smart Power **48**(6), 40–46 (2020)
21. Huang, Y., Yang, P., Liu, Z.: Typical characteristics and engineering design of residential multi-microgrids. Electric Power Eng. Technol. **38**(3), 13–20 (2019)
22. Zhang, Z., Li, H.: A hierarchical energy management strategy for an island microgrid cluster considering flexibility. Power Syst. Protect. Control **48**(20), 97–105 (2020)
23. Qu, J., Wu, X., Yan, K., Zhang, B.: Influence of PV station weak power feature on relay protection of outgoing transmission line. Electric Power Autom. Equip. **35**(5), 146–151 (2015)
24. Yi, Y., Luo, Y., Zhang, Z., Long, X., Wang, D.: Failure analysis and protection scheme of centralized photovoltaic power station convergence system. Electric Power Eng. Technol. **40**(2), 1–10 (2021)
25. Sun, Y., Liu, Y., Fang, J., Zhang, X., Yan, Y., Jiang, X.: Influence of distributed photovoltaic access on fault location in distribution network lines. Smart Power **48**(9), 102–107 (2020)

Optimized Edge-cCCN Based Model for the Detection of DDoS Attack in IoT Environment

Brij B. Gupta[1,2($\boxtimes$)], Akshat Gaurav[3], Kwok Tai Chui[4], and Varsha Arya[5,6]

[1] Department of Computer Science and Information Engineering, Asia University, Taichung 413, Taiwan
gupta.brij@gmail.com
[2] Lebanese American University, Beirut 1102, Lebanon
[3] Ronin Institute, Montclair, NJ 07043, USA
akshat.gaurav@roninstitute.org
[4] School of Science and Technology, Hong Kong Metropolitan University, Kowloon, Hong Kong
jktchui@ouhk.edu.hk
[5] Department of Business Administration, Asia University, Taichung, Taiwan
[6] Insights2Techinfo, New Delhi, India

Abstract. In the context of the Internet of Things (IoT), safeguarding against Distributed Denial of Service (DDoS) attacks is critical. This paper introduces an Optimized Edge-cCNN (Convolutional Neural Network) Model designed for robust DDoS detection in IoT environments. The model employs two specialized CNN layers to identify distinct DDoS attack types. To enhance its performance, we utilize the Cuckoo Search algorithm to fine-tune hyperparameters effectively. Our approach demonstrates superior accuracy compared to existing methods while remaining lightweight, making it suitable for resource-constrained edge devices. Through rigorous evaluation, our model exhibits its effectiveness in real-time DDoS threat mitigation. The Optimized Edge-cCNN Model presents an innovative solution for enhancing IoT security, combining deep learning and optimization techniques to combat evolving DDoS attacks effectively.

Keywords: CNN · DDoS · Edge Computing · IoT · Cuckoo Search

1 Introduction

The development of smart IoT devices has seen significant advancements in recent years [2,14]. The integration of the Internet of Things (IoT) and cloud computing has led to the emergence of consumer-oriented smart IoT devices [6,26]. These devices have the capability to auto-organize, share information, and react to changes in the environment [2]. The rapid development of IoT applications has brought great convenience to people's lives, but it has also introduced security challenges [7]. Many IoT devices have authentication flaws, making them vulnerable to security breaches [7]. To address these challenges, researchers have

J. Feng et al. (Eds.): EDGE 2023, LNCS 14205, pp. 14–23, 2024.
https://doi.org/10.1007/978-3-031-51826-3_2

proposed authentication schemes for large-scale smart IoT applications [7]. Additionally, there has been a growing interest in the development of applications for smart homes using IoT technology [5]. Platforms like SmartThings have been widely used to develop IoT applications that automate the control of devices in homes [5]. The development of smart IoT devices is not limited to smart homes, but also extends to various domains such as industrial automation, healthcare, energy management, and smart cities [1]. However, the increasing number of IoT devices also poses security risks, as malicious activities can be performed through these devices [15, 19]. Therefore, there is a need for robust security measures, including intrusion detection systems, to protect IoT networks [27]. Furthermore, the limited processing and memory capabilities of IoT devices present challenges in implementing security measures [16, 27]. The combination of big data and IoT technologies has also played a major role in the development of smart cities [18, 21]. Overall, the recent development in smart IoT devices has opened up new possibilities for automation, convenience, and improved quality of life, but it has also brought about security challenges that need to be addressed.

A major security concern in the Internet of Things (IoT) context is the Distributed Denial of Service (DDoS) attack [3, 25]. The goal of a DoS attack is to overload the host server with so many requests that it cannot handle the load of genuine users [3]. Because of their low memory and processing power, IoT devices are easy targets for distributed denial of service attacks [13]. These attacks can lead to service interruptions, loss of data, and financial losses [13, 22]. The high number of connected devices that may be hijacked and utilised as part of a botnet is one of the key issues in preventing DDoS assaults in the IoT ecosystem [3]. Attackers can easily exploit the vulnerabilities of IoT devices and control them to launch DDoS attacks [13]. The sheer scale and distributed nature of IoT devices make it difficult to detect and mitigate these attacks effectively [24].

2 Related Work

DDoS attack is not a new attack in the IoT environment [8, 20]. DDoS attack targets the availability of victims resource in the IoT environment. Detecting DDoS attacks in IoT environments poses several challenges. First, owing to the enormous number of connected devices and the lack of adequate resources and security protocols, IoT networks are very susceptible to DDoS assaults [12, 23]. The sheer scale and diversity of IoT devices make it difficult to detect and mitigate attacks effectively. Secondly, traditional security solutions like firewalls and intrusion detection systems are often inadequate for detecting complex DDoS attacks in IoT networks [11, 17]. These solutions typically rely on static predefined rules, which may not be able to accurately identify and filter out attack traffic from normal traffic [11, 29, 30]. Furthermore, the dynamic nature of IoT networks makes it challenging to distinguish between legitimate and malicious traffic. IoT devices generate a vast amount of data, and distinguishing between normal and anomalous behavior requires sophisticated analysis techniques [10]. Machine learning algorithms, such as neural networks, can be used to analyze IoT network traffic and detect DDoS attacks based on IoT-specific network behaviors [9,10].

Another challenge is the impact of DDoS attacks on smart devices. DDoS attacks can disrupt the availability and functionality of IoT devices, leading to service outages and potential damage to physical infrastructure [3,28]. Detecting and mitigating these attacks in real-time is crucial to ensure the uninterrupted operation of IoT systems. Additionally, the implementation of effective DDoS detection and mitigation solutions in IoT environments is complicated by the use of Blockchain technology. While Blockchain has the potential to address DDoS attacks by providing a decentralized and tamper-proof system, there are challenges associated with its implementation in IoT networks [4,23]. These challenges include scalability, resource constraints, and the need for consensus among IoT devices. In summary, the challenges associated with detecting DDoS attacks in IoT environments include the vulnerability of IoT networks, the limitations of traditional security solutions, the dynamic nature of IoT traffic, the impact on IoT services, and the complexities of implementing DDoS detection solutions using Blockchain technology. Overcoming these challenges requires the development of advanced detection techniques, such as machine learning algorithms, and the integration of robust security measures into IoT devices and networks.

3   Proposed Model

In this section, details of our proposed model are explained. As the processing power of smart devices in the IoT environment is less, we implement our proposed approach on the fog node. As in the IoT environment, the edge/fog node has higher processing power than the normal node; our approach did not overlap the edge/fog node. Figure 1 presents the proposed approach for the detection of DDoS attacks in the IoT model. The architecture of the CNN model consists of several key components as represented in Fig. 2:

- **Convolutional Layers**: The model starts with two 1D convolutional layers (conv1 and conv2). The first layer takes input data with 41 features and applies a 1D convolution operation with a kernel size of 1. The second layer processes the output of the first layer and transforms it into a feature space with 128 channels. These convolutional layers are responsible for extracting essential spatial features from the input data.
- **Activation Functions**: After each convolutional layer, a Rectified Linear Unit (ReLU) activation function (relu1 and relu2) is applied to introduce non-linearity into the model and capture complex patterns.
- **Max-Pooling Layers**: Following the activation functions, max-pooling layers (maxpool1 and maxpool2) are employed to downsample the feature maps, reducing the spatial dimensions while preserving important features. These layers help in reducing computational complexity and enhancing the model's robustness.

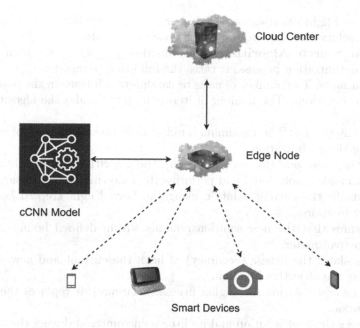

Fig. 1. Proposed Approach

- **Flatten Layer**: After the second max-pooling layer, a flatten layer is used to reshape the data into a one-dimensional vector. This prepares the data for fully connected layers.
- **Fully Connected Layers**: The model includes two fully connected layers (fc1 and fc2). The first fully connected layer has 128 neurons and introduces further non-linearity through a ReLU activation function (relu3). The second fully connected layer has 5 neurons, which typically correspond to the different classes or categories that the model aims to classify the input data into.
- **Dropout Layer**: To prevent overfitting and improve the model's generalization ability, a dropout layer with a dropout rate of 0.5 is added after the third ReLU activation (dropout).

The details of Cuckoo search algorithm are as follows:

- **Objective Function**: This function defines the objective to be optimized by the Cuckoo Search algorithm. In this case, the objective is to maximize the accuracy of the CNN model. The function takes a set of hyperparameters as input (batch size, learning rate, number of filters, and number of epochs), configures the CNN model with these hyperparameters, and trains it on the provided training data. It calculates the accuracy of the model's predictions on the training data and returns this accuracy. The Cuckoo Search algorithm aims to find the hyperparameters that maximize this accuracy.
- **Levy Flight**: This function implements the Levy Flight step, a key component of the Cuckoo Search algorithm. It generates a random step size based

on a Levy Flight distribution. The generated step size is used to perturb the current solution to explore the search space effectively.
- **Cuckoo Search Algorithm**: This function performs the main Cuckoo Search optimization process. It takes the following parameters:
  - num_nests: The number of nests or candidate solutions in the population.
  - num_iterations: The number of iterations (or rounds) the algorithm will run.
  - max_iterations: The maximum number of iterations allowed before stopping the optimization.

Inside the main loop (for each iteration), the algorithm iterates through the nests (candidate solutions) and performs the following steps for each nest:
- Perturbs the current solution using the Levy Flight step to generate a new solution.
- Ensures that the new solution remains within defined bounds for each hyperparameter.
- Calculates the fitness (accuracy) of both the current and new solutions using the objective function.
- If the new solution has higher fitness (accuracy), it replaces the current solution.
- Tracks the best solution and its fitness encountered during the search.

At the end of each iteration, the algorithm prints information about the current iteration, the best solution found so far, and its corresponding accuracy. If the number of iterations reaches or exceeds the max_iterations, the search terminates prematurely.

We also compare the results of our proposed approach with other traditional approaches, Fig. 2 presents this comparison. From Fig. 5 it is clear that our proposed approach detects different types of cyber attacks efficiently.

4   Results and Discussion

Figure 3 represents the loss and accuracy curves for the cCNN deep learning model during training and evaluation, typically for a classification task. The details of the curves are as follows:

- As the epochs progress (from 0 to 9), we can see that both training accuracy (Train acc) and test accuracy (Test acc) increase steadily. This indicates that the model is learning to classify the data more accurately with each epoch, both on the training data and the test data.
- Simultaneously, the training loss (Train loss) decreases, which means that the model is reducing its error when fitting the training data. Lower training loss typically correlates with higher training accuracy.
- Importantly, the test loss (Test loss) also decreases, which is a positive sign of the model's ability to generalize. The decreasing test loss suggests that the model is not overfitting to the training data but is learning to make accurate predictions on unseen data.

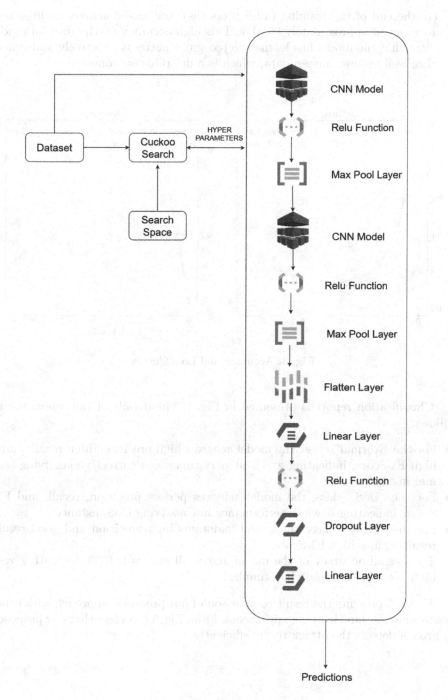

CNN Model

Relu Function

Max Pool Layer

CNN Model

Relu Function

Max Pool Layer

Flatten Layer

Linear Layer

Relu Function

Dropout Layer

Linear Layer

HYPER PARAMETERS

Dataset

Cuckoo Search

Search Space

Predictions

Fig. 2. Proposed Model

By the end of the training (after 9 epochs), the model achieves a high test accuracy of approximately 99.31%. This high accuracy on the test data indicates that the model has learned to recognize patterns effectively and generalize well to new, unseen data, which is a desirable outcome.

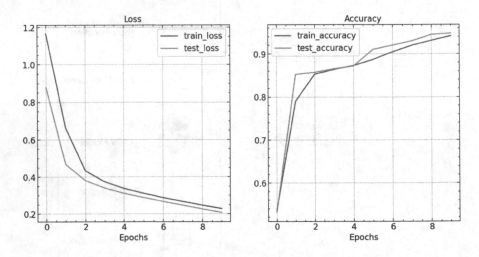

Fig. 3. Accuracy and Loss Curves

Classification report is presented in Fig. 4. The details of the report are as follows:

- For the "Normal" class, the model achieves high precision, high recall, and a high F1-Score, indicating excellent performance in correctly classifying normal instances.
- For the "DoS" class, the model achieves perfect precision, recall, and F1-Score, indicating flawless performance in classifying DoS instances.
- For the "Probe" class, the model maintains high precision and good recall, resulting in a high F1-Score.
- The overall accuracy of the model across all classes is 0.99, indicating very high accuracy in classifying samples.

Figure 5 presents the result comparison of our proposed approach with other traditional machine learning approaches. From Fig. 5 it is clear that our proposed approach detects the attack traffic efficiently.

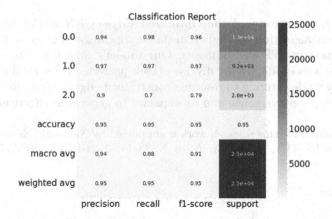

Fig. 4. Classification Report

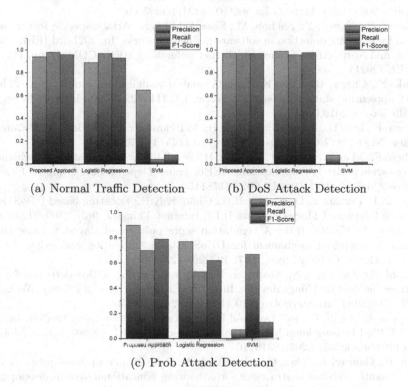

(a) Normal Traffic Detection   (b) DoS Attack Detection

(c) Prob Attack Detection

Fig. 5. Result Comparison

5   Conclusion

In this paper, we introduced the Optimized Edge-cCNN model, utilizing the Cuckoo Search algorithm for hyperparameter optimization, to address DDoS attack detection in IoT environments. Our model's dual CNN layers demonstrated robustness in identifying diverse attack patterns. It excelled in accuracy and efficiency while catering to resource-constrained edge devices. Results showcased the model's convergence and its capacity to generalize effectively.

Acknowledgement. This research work is supported by National Science and Technology Council (NSTC), Taiwan Grant No. NSTC112-2221-E-468-008-MY3.

References

1. Internet of things and wireless sensor network for smart cities. Int. J. Comput. Sci. **14**, 50–55 (2017). https://doi.org/10.20943/01201705.5055
2. Wireless connected smart microsystems. Sens. Mater. 447 (2018). https://doi.org/10.18494/sam.2018.1765
3. Detection and prevention algorithm of DDoS attack over the IoT networks. Tem J. 899–906 (2020). https://doi.org/10.18421/tem93-09
4. Abbas, N., Nasser, Y., Shehab, M., Sharafeddine, S.: Attack-specific feature selection for anomaly detection in software-defined networks. In: 2021 3rd IEEE Middle East and North Africa Communications Conference (MENACOMM), pp. 142–146. IEEE (2021)
5. Bak, N., Chang, B., Choi, K.: SmartVisual: a visualisation tool for SmartThings IoT apps using static analysis. IET Softw. **14**, 411–422 (2020). https://doi.org/10.1049/iet-sen.2019.0344
6. Chen, F., Luo, D., Xiang, T., Truong, H.: IoT cloud security review. ACM Comput. Surv. **54**, 1–36 (2021). https://doi.org/10.1145/3447625
7. Chen, F., Xiao, Z., Xiang, T., Truong, H.: A full lifecycle authentication scheme for large-scale smart IoT applications. IEEE Trans. Depend. Sec. Comput. 1 (2022). https://doi.org/10.1109/tdsc.2022.3178115
8. Cvitić, I., Perakovic, D., Gupta, B.B., Choo, K.K.R.: Boosting-based DDoS detection in Internet of Things systems. IEEE Internet Things J. **9**(3), 2109–2123 (2021)
9. Dahiya, A., Gupta, B.B.: A reputation score policy and Bayesian game theory based incentivized mechanism for DDoS attacks mitigation and cyber defense. Futur. Gener. Comput. Syst. **117**, 193–204 (2021)
10. Doshi, R., Apthorpe, N., Feamster, N.: Machine learning DDoS detection for consumer Internet of Things devices. In: 2018 IEEE Security and Privacy Workshops (SPW) (2018). https://doi.org/10.1109/spw.2018.00013
11. Fayyaz, U., Shah, G.: IoT DoS and DDoS attack detection using ResNet. In: 2020 IEEE 23rd International Multitopic Conference (INMIC) (2020). https://doi.org/10.1109/inmic50486.2020.9318216
12. Hu, B., Gaurav, A., Choi, C., Almomani, A.: Evaluation and comparative analysis of semantic web-based strategies for enhancing educational system development. Int. J. Semant. Web Inform. Syst. (IJSWIS) **18**(1), 1–14 (2022)
13. Khader, R., Eleyan, D.: Survey of DoS/DDoS attacks in IoT. Sustain. Eng. Innov. ISSN 2712–0562 **3**, 23–28 (2021). https://doi.org/10.37868/sei.v3i1.124

14. Khanam, S., Tanweer, S., Khalid, S.S.: Future of internet of things: enhancing cloud-based IoT using artificial intelligence. Int. J. Cloud Appl. Comput. (IJCAC) **12**(1), 1–23 (2022)
15. Kiran, M.A., Pasupuleti, S.K., Eswari, R.: Efficient pairing-free identity-based Signcryption scheme for cloud-assisted IoT. Int. J. Cloud Appl. Comput. (IJCAC) **12**(1), 1–15 (2022)
16. Kumar, R., Singh, S.K., Lobiyal, D., Chui, K.T., Santaniello, D., Rafsanjani, M.K.: A novel decentralized group key management scheme for cloud-based vehicular IoT networks. Int. J. Cloud Appl. Comput. (IJCAC) **12**(1), 1–34 (2022)
17. Mishra, A., Gupta, N., Gupta, B.: Defense mechanisms against DDoS attack based on entropy in SDN-cloud using pox controller. Telecommun. Syst. **77**, 47–62 (2021)
18. Nagpal, N.: Analyzing role of big data and IoT in smart cities. Int. J. Adv. Eng. Manage. Sci. **3**, 584–586 (2017). https://doi.org/10.24001/ijaems.3.5.29
19. Quist, A.: Digital forensic challenges in internet of things (IoT). Adv. Multidiscip. Sci. Res. J. Publ. **1**, 119–124 (2022). https://doi.org/10.22624/aims/crp-bk3-p20
20. Raj, M.G., Pani, S.K.: Chaotic whale crow optimization algorithm for secure routing in the IoT environment. Int. J. Seman. Web Inform. Syst. (IJSWIS) **18**(1), 1–25 (2022)
21. Sadatacharapandi, T.P., Padmavathi, S.: Survey on service placement, provisioning, and composition for fog-based IoT systems. Int. J. Cloud Appl. Comput. (IJCAC) **12**(1), 1–14 (2022)
22. Sarrab, M., Alshohoumi, F.: Assisted-fog-based framework for IoT-based healthcare data preservation. Int. J. Cloud Appl. Comput. (IJCAC) **11**(2), 1–16 (2021)
23. Shah, Z., Ullah, I., Li, H., Levula, A., Khurshid, K.: Blockchain based solutions to mitigate distributed denial of service (DDoS) attacks in the Internet of Things (IoT): a survey. Sensors **22**, 1094 (2022). https://doi.org/10.3390/s22031094
24. Silva, F., Silva, E., Neto, E., Lemos, M., Neto, A., Esposito, F.: A taxonomy of DDoS attack mitigation approaches featured by SDN technologies in IoT scenarios. Sensors **20**, 3078 (2020). https://doi.org/10.3390/s20113078
25. Singh, A., Gupta, B.B.: Distributed denial-of-service (DDoS) attacks and defense mechanisms in various web-enabled computing platforms: issues, challenges, and future research directions. Int. J. Semant. Web Inform. Syst. (IJSWIS) **18**(1), 1–43 (2022)
26. Tiwari, A., Garg, R.: Adaptive ontology-based IoT resource provisioning in computing systems. Int. J. Semant. Web Inform. Syst. (IJSWIS) **18**(1), 1–18 (2022)
27. Ullah, I., Mahmoud, Q.: A two-level flow-based anomalous activity detection system for IoT networks. Electronics **9**, 530 (2020). https://doi.org/10.3390/electronics9030530
28. Wahab, O.A., Bentahar, J., Otrok, H., Mourad, A.: Optimal load distribution for the detection of VM-based DDoS attacks in the cloud. IEEE Trans. Serv. Comput. **13**(1), 114–129 (2017)
29. Wassan, S., et al.: Gradient boosting for health IoT federated learning. Sustainability **14**(24), 16842 (2022)
30. Zhang, Q., Guo, Z., Zhu, Y., Vijayakumar, P., Castiglione, A., Gupta, B.B.: A deep learning-based fast fake news detection model for cyber-physical social services. Pattern Recogn. Lett. **168**, 31–38 (2023)

RuCIL: Enabling Privacy-Enhanced Edge Computing for Federated Learning

Sahil Ashish Nimsarkar$^{(\boxtimes)}$, Ruchir Raj Gupta ,
and Rajesh Balliram Ingle

Dr. Shyama Prasad Mukherjee International Institute of Information Technology,
Naya Raipur, India
{sahiln21102,ruchir21100}@iiitnr.edu.in

Abstract. Federated learning has emerged as a promising approach for collaborative machine learning while preserving data privacy in distributed settings. Despite recent advancements, challenges such as privacy preservation and communication overhead persist, limiting its practical utility. This work proposes a novel model - RuCIL - **R**esource **u**tilization and **C**omputational **I**mpact metric-based model for Edge **L**earning that synergizes federated learning with edge computing, leveraging the computational capabilities of latest edge devices. By doing so, it optimizes privacy-preserving mechanisms and communication overhead of the model. This work not only addresses the limitations of federated learning but also paves the way for more efficient and privacy-conscious machine learning applications in distributed environments.

Keywords: edge computing · federated learning · privacy management · context-awareness · communication overhead · computation

1 Introduction

In the dynamic realm of machine learning, federated learning has surfaced as a groundbreaking methodology with the potential to safeguard data privacy while fostering cooperative model training across distributed settings. This innovative framework orchestrates the distributed collaboration of machine learning models, making it well-suited for resource-constrained edge devices. In this intricate environment, the paramount challenges of privacy preservation, communication optimization, and computational efficiency take center stage, their formidable presence influencing the transformative capacity of federated learning within the landscape of edge computing scenarios.

Edge computing, characterized by the proliferation of resource-constrained devices at the network periphery, presents a unique arena for federated learning to flourish. Edge federated learning harnesses the latent power of smartphones, sensors, and IoT devices, transforming them into intelligent nodes contributing to collective learning. At the heart of this revolution lies the preservation of data privacy, a fundamental concern in an age where information is both invaluable and sensitive.

© The Author(s), under exclusive license to Springer Nature Switzerland AG 2024
J. Feng et al. (Eds.): EDGE 2023, LNCS 14205, pp. 24–36, 2024.
https://doi.org/10.1007/978-3-031-51826-3_3

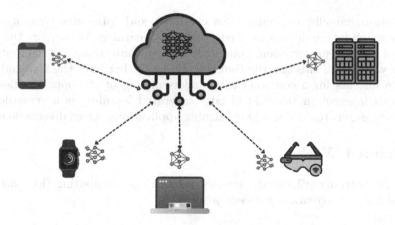

Fig. 1. Federated Learning at Work

As these distributed nodes collaboratively refine machine learning models, preserving the privacy of the data they hold becomes paramount. Edge federated learning seeks to protect the confidentiality of individual datasets while simultaneously improving model accuracy through collaborative efforts. However, beneath this promising paradigm are privacy challenges, ranging from membership inference attacks to data inference attacks. These adversarial maneuvers threaten the sanctity of sensitive data, underscoring the pressing need for robust privacy-preserving mechanisms.

Beyond privacy, the efficacy of edge federated learning hinges on addressing the intricate balance between communication and computation. In cross-device edge federated learning, where millions of low-power nodes with limited data holdings converge, communication bottlenecks become apparent. Balancing the number of communication rounds while optimizing model performance remains a complex problem. Conversely, cross-silo edge federated learning grapples with efficient computation distribution among a relatively small number of nodes, necessitating innovations in network quantization, pruning, and system-level heterogeneity management.

This work embarks on a journey through the realms of edge federated learning, navigating the challenges of privacy preservation, communication efficiency, and computational management. Drawing upon recent advancements and open questions in the field, we propose novel approaches to enhance edge federated learning. Our research seeks to empower this paradigm with practical solutions, transforming it into a potent tool for privacy-conscious and efficient machine learning applications across various domains and leveraging the unique capabilities of edge devices, positioning them as key enablers of efficient information capture.

In the ensuing sections, we delve into the core challenges, existing solutions, the architecture of our proposed framework, presenting empirical evaluations and experimental results that demonstrate its effectiveness in enhancing privacy preservation, reducing communication overhead, and optimizing computational efficiency, and future directions in edge federated learning. We explore the intricacies of privacy preservation, communication optimization, and computation efficiency. Through this contribution, we aim to further pave the way and offer valuable insights for a comprehensive understanding of the opportunities and challenges inherent in the field of edge federated learning as a versatile and privacy-conscious tool for machine learning applications across diverse domains.

2 Related Work

Federated Learning (FL) at the intersection of Edge Computing (EC) has garnered significant attention in recent years.

2.1 Edge Federated Learning

As FL's potential in EC applications becomes increasingly evident, a number of survey studies have been conducted, offering comprehensive insights into various use cases and challenges that this dynamic field presents [1]- [5]. FL harnesses the computational capabilities of edge servers and the vast network of edge devices, making it a potent technology for EC network optimization [1].

Researchers have meticulously investigated FL's potential, addressing the unique challenges it presents in EC contexts. These challenges encompass communication and computation efficiency, device heterogeneity, privacy and security concerns, client selection, resource allocation, and service pricing [2,3].

As a response, comprehensive solutions have been proposed, offering valuable insights into overcoming hurdles and ensuring the successful deployment of FL at the edge [4]. Additionally, real-world case studies in domains such as smart healthcare and Unmanned Aerial Vehicles (UAVs) highlight the practical applicability of FL within EC environments.

A systematic literature review [5] further consolidates these insights, providing a comprehensive overview of FL's integration into the EC paradigm and pointing toward potential avenues for future research. In this dynamic intersection of FL and EC, researchers and practitioners are poised to advance the field, leveraging FL's capabilities to address privacy concerns, enhance communication efficiency, and unlock innovative applications with profound implications.

2.2 Computation Algorithms

Lachner et al. [6] introduced a context-aware privacy model using Role-Based Access Control (RBAC) mechanisms for edge computing. This model processed sensitive data closer to users, incorporating environmental context in privacy considerations. It lightened centralized cloud systems' load, improving data locality management. Context-aware edge devices enabled early policy establishment by identifying various system contexts and addressing privacy concerns. However, scalability issues could lead to data leakages if the Centralized Context-Oriented Policy (CO-OP) processor became overwhelmed with numerous device connections. Addressing scalability is crucial for maintaining robust data privacy in context-aware privacy enforcement.

In their research [7], Sirigu et al. introduced the ConPrEF framework tailored for edge computing. It allows users to set their privacy boundaries based on context and prevents inadvertent data sharing among users on the same edge node. This is achieved through a technique called Private Set Intersection Cardinality (PSI-CA), protecting privacy by revealing only set size, not individual identities. However, PSI-CA introduces some communication overhead that may affect network efficiency and responsiveness. Additionally, ConPrEF relies on maintaining user lists and preferences, potentially causing storage issues in resource-constrained edge devices.

To bridge the gap between the constrained computational resources of edge devices and the stringent latency requirements, a reinforcement learning-based decision engine [8] was introduced. This engine autonomously configures deep neural networks (DNNs) considering runtime context. Leveraging hybrid edge-cloud deployment and flexible DNN architectures, it creates a model tree offline. In the online phase, it dynamically assembles DNN models in response to changing contexts. Real-world evaluations demonstrate its effectiveness, achieving a notable 30%–50% latency reduction with a marginal 1% accuracy loss. This surpasses baseline methods, highlighting the potential of the RL-based decision engine to enhance edge computing performance under variable conditions.

Ma et al. [9] presented FedSA, a semi-asynchronous federated learning mechanism for heterogeneous edge computing. They establish FedSA's convergence and devise an efficient algorithm for worker participation, extending it to dynamic scenarios and multiple tasks. Experiments on diverse datasets show FedSA's effectiveness in addressing edge heterogeneity, non-IID data, and communication constraints. However, it introduces communication overhead during model transfers and may face challenges with extremely diverse datasets. Achieving scalability in large-scale edge computing scenarios necessitates further optimization.

LSFL [10], a lightweight and secure federated learning scheme for edge nodes, prioritizing privacy preservation and Byzantine robustness. They introduced the Lightweight Two-Server Secure Aggregation protocol, utilizing two servers to enhance security against Byzantine nodes and enable secure model aggregation. LSFL maintains data privacy while achieving classification accuracy similar to FedAvg. Experimental results demonstrated LSFL's fidelity, security, and efficiency without added computational overhead, making it practical for privacy-preserving edge computing federated learning applications.

EdgeFed [11], a novel approach for edge federated learning that separates the local model update process, reducing computational costs for mobile devices. Mobile device outputs are aggregated on the edge server to enhance learning efficiency and reduce global communication frequency. Empirical experiments demonstrated EdgeFed's effectiveness across various bandwidth scenarios, significantly lowering computational costs for both mobile devices and global communication compared to FedAvg. Additionally, optimization algorithms tailored for federated learning on edge computing platforms were proposed, further addressing the challenge of high computational costs on mobile devices. The division of local updates between mobile devices and the edge server, followed by global aggregation, resulted in significant cost reductions for mobile devices. These findings provide valuable insights into parameter selection in different bandwidth conditions.

2.3   Network Layer Algorithms

The TCP/IP Protocol stands as the foundational framework underpinning modern networking and serves as the backbone of the internet. TCP/IP comprises a suite of communication protocols that facilitate the efficient and reliable transfer of data across interconnected networks. With its multi-layered structure, TCP/IP standardizes various aspects of data transmission, including addressing, routing, and error handling. This suite's widespread adoption has cemented its role in our digital lives, supporting a wide array of applications, such as web browsing, email, and file transfers.

At its core, edge computing, which empowers data processing at or near the data source, TCP/IP remains a crucial player, facilitating the convergence of distributed computing and networking. It assumes a pivotal role in ensuring connectivity, low-latency data transfer, scalability, security, and interoperability across diverse edge devices and sensors.

However, it's important to note some of TCP/IP's limitations, including susceptibility to security threats like DDoS attacks and packet sniffing, which can jeopardize data security. Furthermore, TCP/IP's original design for a stable and predictable internet landscape may not seamlessly align with the dynamic and heterogeneous nature of contemporary edge computing environments. The protocol's resource-intensive nature could lead to inefficiencies in low-power edge devices, and it may require optimization to meet the stringent latency demands of real-time edge applications.

In their paper, Ouyang et al. [12] introduced the choice of message communication libraries which is crucial for optimizing the performance of different parameter server systems and Allreduce algorithms. Typically, these systems are implemented using communication libraries like ZeroMQ and gRPC. ZeroMQ is known for its high performance and low-latency asynchronous messaging capabilities, while gRPC is a powerful remote procedure call (RPC) framework developed by Google.

gRPC [16] can play a crucial role in facilitating Edge Federated Learning when built on top of the TCP/IP protocol stack. Edge FL involves training machine learning models on edge devices, such as smartphones, IoT devices, or edge servers, while preserving data privacy and minimizing the need for centralized data transfer. It provides efficient, low-latency communication suitable for real-time collaborative training among edge devices. Its support for multiple programming languages ensures flexibility and interoperability in diverse edge environments. Additionally, gRPC's built-in authentication and encryption mechanisms enhance security, protecting sensitive federated learning data during transmission.

However, gRPC in Edge Federated Learning has limitations, including resource intensity, latency, complexity, compatibility, network overhead, security, scaling, and error handling. These factors should be carefully considered when implementing gRPC in Edge FL applications to ensure optimal performance, especially in resource-constrained edge environments where efficient and low-latency communication is essential for real-time federated learning tasks.

ZeroMQ [15], often abbreviated as ØMQ, is a lightweight and high-performance messaging protocol that plays a pivotal role in Edge Federated Learning. This protocol facilitates efficient and low-latency communication between distributed edge devices and servers, making it an ideal choice for real-time federated learning tasks. With its minimalistic design and focus on asynchronous messaging patterns, ØMQ minimizes resource overhead while ensuring reliable data exchange in dynamic and resource-constrained edge computing environments. Its versatility and support for various programming languages enhance its suitability for Edge FL applications, enabling seamless communication between edge nodes and central servers for collaborative machine learning tasks.

Table 1 provides a summary of the comparison of our proposed model to existing models.

Table 1. Comparison of our proposed method to current state-of-the-art works.

References	Title	Privacy	Communication Overhead	Computation	Context Aware	Federated Learning
[6]	Context-aware enforcement of privacy policies in EC	Y	X	X	Y	X
[7]	Context-based privacy enforcement framework for EC	Y	X	Y	Y	X
[8]	Context-aware deep model compression for EC computing	X	Y	X	Y	X
[9]	Semi-asynchronous FL mechanism in heterogeneous EC	Y	Y	Y	X	Y
[10]	Lightweight and secure FL scheme for EC	Y	Y	Y	X	Y
[11]	Optimized FL based on EC	X	Y	Y	X	Y
[12]	Communication optimization strategies for distributed DNN training	X	Y	X	X	X
Our Work	RuCIL - based approach	Y	Í	Y	Y	Y

3 Dataset

MIMIC-III (Medical Information Mart for Intensive Care III) [14] is a crucial resource in the realm of medical research, especially in critical care and medical informatics. It contains de-identified health records from over 40,000 patients at the Beth Israel Deaconess Medical Center in Boston, spanning from 2001 to 2012. This dataset includes a wide range of clinical data, from demographics to vital signs, lab results, medications, and clinical notes. The detailed information about patients in intensive care units makes MIMIC-III invaluable for our research in developing privacy-preserving mechanisms in federated learning.

Given the sensitive nature of the data in MIMIC-III, it's essential to create models that rigorously protect privacy. When we engage in privacy-preserving federated learning with this dataset, our main goal is to advance machine learning models while ensuring the utmost security of patient information. Developing robust, ethical, and privacy-conscious methods isn't an option but a necessity. MIMIC-III serves as a crucial testing ground for cultivating these vital methods, guaranteeing that progress in medical research and machine learning is not only innovative but also upholds the highest standards of patient confidentiality and data privacy.

4 Proposed Metric

Based on prior research, the exploration of privacy-preserving methods within the context of context awareness has become a well-studied field. Previous studies have examined the complex challenges of protecting privacy while considering the context of data transactions. However, the existing literature highlights a significant limitation-namely, the diverse nature of devices in the federated learning environment. These devices vary greatly in terms of computing power and network capabilities, creating a formidable challenge in designing a flexible architectural framework that can effectively accommodate such diversity. To tackle this challenge successfully, it's clear that privacy-preserving methods must consider the dynamic interaction between context awareness and the diverse characteristics of devices in federated learning scenarios. Developing a comprehensive solution requires innovative strategies to harmonize the differing computational capacities and network infrastructures, ultimately creating a resilient privacy-preserving architecture.

Henceforth, building upon this premise, we advocate for the introduction of a novel metric RuCIL - **R**esource **u**tilization and **C**omputational **I**mpact metric for Edge **L**earning designed to ameliorate the existing challenges. This metric aims to address the complexities associated with scoring an edge device's proficiency in hosting machine learning models within the dynamic context of a federated learning environment, while simultaneously adhering to the requisite privacy constraints. The proposed metric strategically optimizes the interplay between computational power and privacy-preserving procedures across a predefined spectrum. This spectrum is discretized into 'm' distinct sections, where sections proximate to 1 epitomize a higher degree of privacy enablement, while those closer to 'm' embody a more conservative approach with a focus on computational efficiency. In the interest of flexibility, we consider multiple values for 'm,' and after careful consideration, we designate 'm=4' as the default value for this dataset. This choice aligns with a balance that accommodates varying privacy needs and computational capacities within the federated learning landscape, offering a practical and adaptable approach to assess the privacy-enabling capabilities of edge devices.

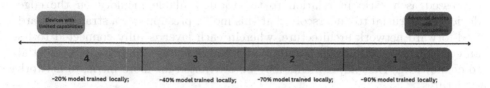

Fig. 2. Segmenting devices for privacy by processing power

This concept originates from the realization that not all edge devices have the computing power to run resource-intensive deep-learning models locally. To tackle this challenge, it's crucial to not only address the limitations of edge devices but also ensure the privacy of models that can execute demanding algorithms. Recent research by Pustozerova and others highlights the significant risk of information leakage in deep-learning models, potentially exposing data even with strong privacy measures in place.

In response to this inherent challenge, a pivotal approach is taken to ensure the preservation of privacy. Each segment within the federated learning environment is tasked with constructing and training its own dedicated neural network. This network is derived from a master training model, and its exclusive purpose is to facilitate the training and subsequent updates of weights and biases pertinent to that specific segment. This segmentation strategy is strategically employed to mitigate the risks associated with information leakage across hidden layers, thereby fortifying the privacy preservation mechanisms within the federated learning framework. By decentralizing the training process to segment-specific neural networks, we aim to enhance the robustness of the system and minimize the potential for unintended data leakage, aligning with the overarching goal of safeguarding the privacy of sensitive information processed within the federated learning paradigm.

This function has been intricately designed to furnish an approximation of the memory requisites for a neural network. It comprehensively considers several factors, including the sizes of individual layers, the dimensions of the input data for the initial layer, the number of samples present in the dataset, and the specified data type utilized for value storage. The function initializes a computes the memory required for a single input sample forwarded into the network. Employing a sum function that computes for over each layer size, the function dynamically computes the number of weights, biases, and activations for each layer, taking into consideration the entirety of the dataset.

Within this iterative process, 't' represents the size of the specified data type in bytes (e.g., float32, float64). The function proceeds to calculate the total memory requirement for parameters (weights and biases) and activations for each layer. The computed memory for each layer is progressively added to the running total, concurrently updating the input size for the subsequent layer.

The ultimate objective of this function is to yield the cumulative estimated memory required for the entire neural network. This calculated total is then expressed as a ratio in relation to the total available memory on the edge device. It is crucial to underscore that this model presupposes a straightforward feed-forward network architecture, wherein each layer is fully connected to its antecedent layer. While this assumption accommodates simplicity, it's essential to acknowledge that adjustments may be warranted for more intricate network structures.

The RuCIL metric (ϕ) is then calculated from this formula :

$$\phi = \frac{t \cdot \sum_{i=1}^{\theta}(H_i^n + H_i^n \cdot U + H_i^n \cdot V)}{\eta} \tag{1}$$

where:

θ is derived from following equation (2)

n is the total number of hidden layers in the neural network

t is the size of the data type used to store values

U is the number of elements in the input layer

V is the total number of elements in the training dataset

H^n is a $(1 \times n)$ matrix of neurons in the hidden layers

η is the available memory on the edge device

Here, θ is computed from this formula:

$$\theta = \begin{cases} n - (c-1) & \text{if } n < m \\ n - (c-1) \cdot \lfloor \frac{n}{m} \rfloor & \text{if } n \geq m \end{cases} \tag{2}$$

where:

n is the total number of hidden layers in the neural network

m is the number of segments specified for the metric (default m = 4)

c is the segment enforced for the edge device

This formula introduces a pivotal necessity condition for the designated segment protocol, mandating that the RuCIL score must unequivocally be less than 1. This stringent criterion is imposed to ensure the efficacy and appropriateness of the segment protocol in question. However, drawing insights from a comprehensive study conducted by Narendran [18], it is observed that a RuCIL score falling within the range of 0.3 to 0.7 is highly preferred for optimal performance and seamless functionality of the model on the edge device. This empirically derived range signifies a balance that fosters both robustness and efficiency in the operation of the model within the edge device ecosystem. As such, the study's findings serve as a valuable reference point, guiding the establishment of RuCIL score thresholds that align with the pragmatic and effective deployment of the federated learning model on diverse edge devices.

Subsequent to the segmentation process, individuals possessing their personal information will be afforded the capability to execute operations such as creating, reading, updating, or deleting their respective data within the system. In contrast, individuals within specific roles, including medical practitioners, administrative staff, and those possessing requisite clearance levels corresponding to the designated segment, will be restricted to performing read-only operations on the inferences derived from this data. It is imperative to underscore that, at no juncture, can the information stored within edge devices be accessed or retrieved by any individual other than the user to whom it pertains. This stringent access control framework not only safeguards the privacy of individual data but also ensures that access privileges align with the roles and responsibilities of authorized personnel within the federated learning environment. The delineation of access rights serves as a fundamental tenet in fortifying the privacy-preserving measures inherent in the system, fostering a secure and ethically sound data management paradigm within the federated learning framework.

Applying the insights garnered from the preceding discussion, we have endeavored to construct a sample neural network that incorporates a depth of 8 hidden layers. The size of each hidden layer is intentionally varied to accommodate the characteristics of the input dataset. The representation of this neural network is provided below, with the understanding that its presentation serves exclusively for educational purposes. This illustrative example aims to demonstrate the application of the acquired knowledge in the practical development of a neural network architecture, showcasing the relevance of the discussed concepts in a tangible context. The presented network structure, while crafted for educational elucidation, embodies the principles discussed and underscores their applicability in the domain of neural network design within the given dataset parameters.

It is crucial to note that, in the context of the presented image, denoting a particular level 'n,' all data antecedent to this level will be retained and undergo local training. The rationale behind this approach is to confine the training process to the local domain, specifically within the boundary of the designated segment. Notably, the local weights associated with this training will be exclusively updated through neural networks aligned with the corresponding segment. This stringent protocol is implemented meticulously to mitigate the potential risks associated with information leakage. By strictly restricting updates to the neural networks of the matching segment, we aim to fortify the privacy preservation

HIDDEN LAYERS

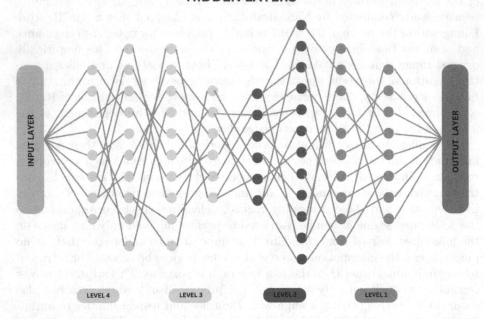

Fig. 3. A RuCIL-Enabled Federated Neural Network

mechanisms inherent in the federated learning system. This procedural safeguard ensures that the information encapsulated in local weights remains insulated and secure from any inadvertent data leakage, thereby upholding the confidentiality and privacy of the federated learning paradigm.

5 Further Use Cases

RuCIL finds versatile applications in various domains, enhancing the performance and privacy of edge computing systems. In the context of industrial predictive maintenance, RuCIL aids in developing context-aware models for edge devices operating within diverse industrial environments. These models consider the unique contextual factors, allowing real-time predictions of machinery failures while maintaining data privacy. The technology not only improves operational efficiency but also safeguards sensitive data in industrial settings.

In precision agriculture, RuCIL enables collaborative analysis of crop conditions and environmental data by edge devices equipped with sensors. By calculating context-aware models, RuCIL ensures privacy-preserving crop analysis, including monitoring soil quality, crop health, and irrigation requirements. This application optimizes agricultural practices by making data-driven insights accessible while respecting data privacy.

6   Conclusion

This research paper introduced a novel framework that combined federated learning with edge computing, addressing persistent challenges in privacy preservation and communication overhead. Leveraging the computational capabilities of edge devices, the proposed framework optimized privacy-preserving mechanisms and enhanced communication efficiency. By doing so, it not only mitigated the limitations of federated learning but also paved the way for more efficient and privacy-conscious machine learning applications in distributed environments. The research delved into the complexities of privacy preservation, communication optimization, and computational management, offering innovative solutions and insights to propel the field of edge federated learning. As the convergence of federated learning and edge computing evolves, this work provided valuable contributions to foster secure, efficient, and privacy-aware machine learning applications across diverse domains.

Despite of all the advances produced in this paper, we recognize that some of our work can be further improved upon, some of which include:

Dependency on Central Server for Some Users: A limitation of the framework is that users lacking devices capable of ensuring Segment 1 privacy may need to rely on the central server. This centralization could potentially affect scalability and fault tolerance.

Need for Reliable Network Layer Protocols: The use of ZeroMQ, while flexible, may resort to less reliable protocols like UDP in edge cases. This raises concerns about consistent data transmission in unpredictable network conditions, necessitating further research into reliable network layer protocols.

References

1. Ju, W., et al.: A survey on federated learning: challenges and applications. International Journal of Machine Learning and Cybernetics, vol. 14, no. 2, Springer Science+Business Media, Nov. 2022, pp. 513–35. https://doi.org/10.1007/s13042-022-01647-y
2. Zhou, Z., Chen, X., Li, E., Zeng, L., Luo, K., Zhang, J.: Edge intelligence: paving the last mile of artificial intelligence with edge computing. Proc. IEEE **107**(8), 1738–1762 (2019). https://doi.org/10.1109/JPROC.2019.2918951
3. Brecko, A., Kajati, E., Koziorek, J., Zolotova, I.: Federated learning for edge computing: a survey. Appl. Sci. **12**, 9124 (2022). https://doi.org/10.3390/app12189124
4. Xia, Qi, et al.: A survey of federated learning for edge computing: research problems and solutions. High-Confidence Comput., **1**(1), 100008 Elsevier BV, June (2021) . https://doi.org/10.1016/j.hcc.2021.100008
5. Abreha, H G., Hayajneh, M., Serhani, M.A.: Federated learning in edge computing: a systematic survey. Sensors. **22**, 450 (2022). https://doi.org/10.3390/s22020450
6. Lachner, C., Rausch, T., Dustdar, S.: Context-Aware Enforcement of Privacy Policies in Edge Computing. In: 2019 IEEE International Congress on Big Data (BigDataCongress), Milan, Italy, 2019, pp. 1-6, https://doi.org/10.1109/BigDataCongress.2019.00014

7. Sirigu, G., Carminati, B., Ferrari, E.: ConPrEF: a context-based privacy enforcement framework for edge computing. In: 2023 IEEE International Conference on Edge Computing and Communications (EDGE), Chicago, IL, USA, 2023, pp. 72–78, https://doi.org/10.1109/EDGE60047.2023.00022
8. Wang, L., et al.: Context-aware deep model compression for edge cloud computing. In: 2020 IEEE 40th International Conference on Distributed Computing Systems (ICDCS), Singapore, Singapore, 2020, pp. 787–797, https://doi.org/10.1109/ICDCS47774.2020.00101
9. Ma, Q., Xu, Y., Xu, H., Jiang, Z., Huang, L., Huang, H.: FedSA: a semi-asynchronous federated learning mechanism in heterogeneous edge computing. IEEE J. Sel. Areas Commun. **39**(12), 3654–3672 (2021). https://doi.org/10.1109/JSAC.2021.3118435
10. Zhang, Z., et al.: LSFL: a lightweight and secure federated learning scheme for edge computing. IEEE Trans. Inform. Foren. Security **18**, 365-379 (2023). https://doi.org/10.1109/TIFS.2022.3221899
11. Ye, Y., Li, S., Liu, F., Tang, Y., Hu, W.: EdgeFed: optimized federated learning based on edge computing. IEEE Access **8**, 209191–209198 (2020). https://doi.org/10.1109/ACCESS.2020.3038287
12. Ouyang, S., et al.: Communication optimization strategies for distributed deep neural network training: a survey. J. Parallel Distrib. Computi. **149**, 52–65 Elsevier BV (Mar 2021). https://doi.org/10.1016/j.jpdc.2020.11.005
13. Wang, Y., Xu, Y., Shi, Q., Chang, T.H.: Quantized federated learning under transmission delay and outage constraints. IEEE J. Selected Areas Commun. **40**(1) 323–341 (2021). https://doi.org/10.1109/JSAC.2021.3126081
14. Johnson, A.E.W., et al.: MIMIC-III, a freely accessible critical care database. Sci. Data **3**, 160035 (2016)
15. Hintjens, P., et al.: ZeroMQ. ZeroMQ Message Transport Protocol, 4.3.4. https://rfc.zeromq.org/spec/23/. Accessed 7 Oct 2023
16. Google Inc. "gRPC." gRPC: A High Performance, Open Source Universal RPC Framework, https://grpc.io/. Accessed 7 Oct 2023
17. Pustozerova, A., Mayer, R.: Information leaks in federated learning. In: Information Leaks in Federated Learning Network and Distributed System Security (NDSS) Symposium (2020). www.ndss-symposium.org/wp-content/uploads/2020/04/diss2020-23004-paper.pdf
18. Mahendran, N.: Analysis of memory consumption by neural networks based on hyperparameters (2021)

Designing Blended Learning Activities in the Era of Artificial Intelligence

Lamei Xu[✉]

Shenzhen Institute of Information Technology, Shenzhen 518172, China
xulamei2013@163.com

Abstract. Effective design of blended learning activities is pivotal to achieve desired learning outcomes. Utilizing the community of inquiry framework, we delve into the strategies for blended learning activities tailored for general elective courses in higher vocational college. At the beginning of these courses, emphasis should be placed on fostering a social presence and cultivating trust and a sense of belonging between teachers and learners, thereby nurturing a conducive learning environment. Midway through the course, the priority shifts to establishing a teaching presence, steering students towards efficacious learning while spurring them to enhance and refine project content. At the final of the course, the focus should pivot to reinforcing cognitive presence, championing comprehensive articulation, self-development and assessment. Typical examples underscore that a project-driven approach to blended learning activity design in higher vocational elective courses markedly bolsters students' advanced cognitive functions, learning efficacy, and interpersonal relationships.

Keywords: Blended Learning · Learning Activity Design · Community of Inquiry

1 Introduction

In the wake of advancements in artificial intelligence technology, blended learning has emerged as a prominent paradigm in the educational sector. While governments and educational institutions are amplifying their focus on and advocacy for blended instruction, higher education institutions are positively driving reforms in blended pedagogy. Nevertheless, China's foray into blended education remains nascent, leaving teachers bereft of effective guidance and confronting a plethora of challenges and impediments. Higher vocational elective courses serve as pivotal conduits for vocational students to broaden their knowledge horizons and enhance their holistic competencies. However, the conventional pedagogical approaches employed in these courses tend to be monolithic and deficient in hands-on application and innovation, thereby failing to ignite students' zeal and enthusiasm for learning. These shortcomings not only deter students' academic outcomes and professional trajectories but also impede the enhancement of the quality and overall prowess of vocational institutions. Notably, the champions of blended pedagogical reforms in vocational colleges are predominantly young teachers.

J. Feng et al. (Eds.): EDGE 2023, LNCS 14205, pp. 37–45, 2024.
https://doi.org/10.1007/978-3-031-51826-3_4

Their limited teaching experience renders them ill-equipped to overhaul the instructional design framework at a macroscopic scale, amplifying the exigency to craft a pragmatic and comprehensive learning activity design strategy at the micro level. Consequently, the imperative to adeptly design blended learning activities has ascended to the forefront of educational discourse. The specific research objective of the paper is investigating the effectiveness of blended learning activities in higher vocational elective courses. This research proposes a project-driven strategy for designing blended learning activities by artificial intelligence technology tailored to higher vocational elective courses. This micro-level approach delineates guidelines to assist teachers in blended learning activities. The overarching goal is to amplify students' learning outcomes and professional competencies, foster their autonomy in learning and collaborative skills, and concurrently bolster the comprehensive institutional excellence of vocational colleges.

2   Theory

2.1   Community of Inquiry Framework

Community of Inquiry Framework.   Introduced in 2001 by Garrison et al., the Community of Inquiry (CoI) framework has evolved into a globally recognized theoretical foundation, guiding blended learning practices. Validated by numerous empirical studies worldwide, this framework posits that effective learning is realized when three interdependent core elements, namely cognitive presence, social presence, and teaching presence, are optimally engaged. The model that can be seen in Fig. 1 asserts that genuine learning emerges only when these three presences are highly active. Dialogue and communication serve as vital channels to foster collaborative engagement, while cultivating a familiar learning milieu lays the groundwork for a conducive learning ambiance. Central to this is steering the learning content, which is pivotal for achieving meaningful learning outcomes. Over the years, the CoI framework has solidified its position as a pivotal theoretical guide for both designing and assessing blended learning activities. This model demystifies the theoretical structure and educational objectives integral to blended learning activity design. All designed learning activities should pivot around the three foundational elements: establishing social presence, bolstering teaching presence, or strengthening cognitive presence.

Garrison D R, Anderson T, Archer W. The first decade of the community of inquiry framework: A retrospective[J]. The internet and higher education, 2010, 13(1–2): 5–9.

2.2   Dynamic Scaffolding Model

Dynamic Scaffolding Model.   Many theoretical and empirical studies have led scholars like Feng Xiaoying to build on the theory of the community of inquiry. This has led to the creation of a dynamic scaffolding model for blended instruction, which can be seen in Fig. 1. This model posits that throughout the three stages of blended learning, teachers ought to craft learning activities with varying degrees of social, teaching, and cognitive presence. Such designs are tailored to cater to the evolving learning characteristics of students at each stage and address pivotal challenges.

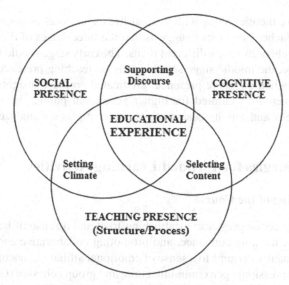

Fig. 1. Community of Inquiry Framework

Initially, during the course's onset, which spans two weeks, the primary objective is to acclimate learners to the online educational environment and foster a sense of belonging and trust within the learning community. The middle of the course is the main stage of course learning, which varies according to the duration of the course. Teachers guide students to overcome the major difficulties in a purposeful and targeted manner. The final four weeks, or the latter segment, aim to consolidate learners' effective learning outcomes.

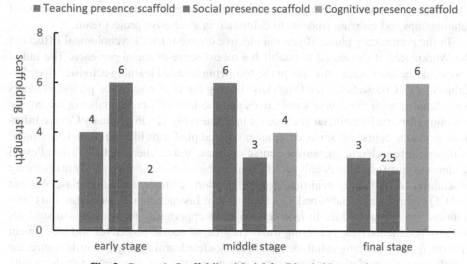

Fig. 2. Dynamic Scaffolding Model for Blended Instruction

Using the above theories along with the real-life experiences of young higher vocational education teachers, this paper suggests that the three stages of the community of inquiry theory should each have a different focus. The early stage should focus on building social presence, the middle stage should focus on teaching presence, and the final stage should strengthen cognitive presence. Predicated on these insights, we designed blended learning activities tailored for higher vocational public elective courses. In addition, the strategy and activity design of typical examples are analyzed.

3 Design Strategies for Blended Learning Activities

3.1 The Beginning of the Course

Prioritize fostering social presence: establishing trust and a sense of belonging, cultivating a conducive learning ambiance, and promoting collaborative endeavors. Social presence predominantly pertains to a sense of emotional affiliation, encompassing three facets: affective expression, open communication, and group cohesion (Garrison, 2010). In the blended learning landscape of general elective courses in higher vocational college, a notable trend is the minimal online interaction and discourse among students. This can be attributed to the online learning milieu that segregates learners, placing each in a virtual silo, which promotes feelings of alienation and isolation. Concurrently, during the initial face-to-face sessions of general elective courses, interdisciplinary students often grapple with establishing mutual trust during their inaugural interactions, making collaborative endeavors challenging. Absent a positive emotional connection and constructive learning disposition towards the course cohort, students might exhibit reluctance or even aversion to upcoming learning engagements. Thus, in the preliminary phase of the blended learning, teachers should emphasize building social presence, facilitating an early establishment of trust and belonging among students. This aids in crafting a trusting environment, fostering a communicative community, developing interpersonal relationships and spurring students to culminate in a cohesive project team.

In the preliminary phase of general elective course titled "Psychological Effects in the Workplace," it's essential to establish a robust sense of social presence. The initial two weeks before course onset adopt the following blended learning activities (listed as Table 1): (1). Course Selection Overview: During the course selection period, students were familiar with the course's objectives and the teacher's credentials via the course selection platform by artificial intelligence machine reply. (2). Preliminary Course Information: As the course commenced, teacher utilized platforms like the 'Rain Classroom' to disseminate welcome messages, course outlines, and teacher's details. This allowed students to grasp essential details such as course objectives and online platform operating procedures. Additionally, real-time communication channels, including class WeChat and QQ groups, were established. (3). Face-to-face Instruction to Foster Trust and Community: The inaugural face-to-face session is an opportunity for teacher and students to introduce themselves, bolstering trust. They detail course objectives and assessment criteria, igniting learning enthusiasm and setting clear learning targets. Furthermore, the significance of completing online assignments is underscored, acquainting students with the blended learning milieu and fueling their zeal for education. In the subsequent face-to-face session, teacher related topics to daily work scenarios, pose guiding queries, and leverage basic tasks to bridge the gap among group members, engendering an interest in prevalent issues like workplace psychology. (4). Promoting a Collaborative Online Learning Atmosphere: In the online realm, teachers orchestrate "group-building" ice-breaker exercises. Here, team members voluntarily associate, collaboratively decide on team monitors, and share details about their academic specializations, hobbies, and competencies. A sense of community is fostered through the appointment of team leaders and teaching aides. Initial roles and collaborative duties for teaching assistants, team leaders, and team members are delineated. Such initiatives facilitate the creation of a blended learning environment rooted in trust, ensuring risk-free interactions and laying the foundation for a thriving learning community.

Table 1. Typical Examples of Blended Learning Activity Design at the Beginning of the Course

Activities	Strategies	Style
Course Description	Familiarize with blended learning environments	Online/offline
Teacher Self-introductions	Build trust	Online/offline
Formation of Class Groups	Build an emotional sense of belonging	Online
Team Establishment	Establish a sense of belonging and create a positive learning atmosphere	Online/offline
Icebreaker Exercises	Establish a sense of belonging and create a positive learning atmosphere	Online/offline
Clarifying goals and standards	Stimulate interest and motivation to learn	Online/offline
Simple Project	Stimulate interest and motivation to learn	Offline

3.2 Mid-Course Phase

The emphasis during this phase is on cultivating a sense of teaching presence: steering students towards efficient learning, fostering both individual and collective knowledge acquisition, and ensuring sustained student engagement. The dimension of teaching presence encompasses three facets: curriculum design and structuring, facilitating discourse, and direct pedagogical intervention. As the course progresses into its primary content delivery phase, it becomes imperative to facilitate students in deepening their understanding, thereby fostering profound learning. Significantly, students' enthusiasm for project-centric learning and a greater propensity for intra-group collaboration increase during the intermediate phase of blended instruction in higher vocational elective courses. However, as the intricacy of learning intensifies and projects demand comprehensive integration and problem resolution, students often exhibit signs of fatigue. This manifests in diminishing morale and a dwindling sense of accomplishment. At this juncture, students often grapple with waning learning motivation, exhibiting symptoms like inattentiveness during lectures, settling for superficial comprehension, mounting academic stress, and developing an aversion or apprehension towards learning. Consequently, it's crucial for teachers, during this phase, to prioritize fostering a robust sense of teaching presence. This can be achieved by devising project-driven instructional methodologies, propelling student groups towards collaborative inquiries—both online and offline—and maintaining student engagement through direct interventions that address and resolve learning challenges.

For the higher vocational elective course titled "Probability in the Game", a pronounced sense of teaching presence is cultivated during the mid-course phase (spanning weeks 3–10). The blended learning activity design for this period entails (listed as Table 2): (1). Project-Driven Instructional Organization: Online Instruction and Direction: Teachers address students' queries related to the subject matter. Concurrently, they curate project themes aligned with the teaching content, supply game design plan exemplars, and oversee group-based game plan formulations.

Offline Instruction: On a weekly basis, teachers elucidate specific probability concepts, and biweekly, they engage students in hands-on probability game sessions. (2). Fostering Individual and Collective Knowledge Acquisition: In individual weeks, teachers provide in-person instruction on specific statistical topics, for instance, "conditional probability". Online, groups are tasked with formulating games such as the "Monty Hall problem". Group roles are delineated, collaborative game plans are crafted, and teachers offer both online and offline guidance, ensuring the refinement of the initial game plan drafts. (3). Project Showcase Sessions to Bolster Continued Engagement: Biweekly, teachers coordinate sessions where project design teams demonstrate their themed games. The sequence follows: The project team's spokesperson presents the design rationale. The game's rule video is showcased, followed by the teacher elucidating pivotal rules and recording criteria. Participating teams play the game, document the process, and, under the mentorship of the design team, decode the game's rules. The gameplay is then analyzed for underlying probability and statistical concepts. The group host announces the game's outcomes, sharing insights on the gameplay, results, and associated probability concepts. The teacher subsequently provides feedback on the game's execution and its thematic alignment. (4). Homework Assignments: After class, students are required to submit online assignments pertinent to the discussed topic. Teachers assess and guide students on these assignments, both online and offline, perpetually kindling their learning enthusiasm.

3.3 The Conclusion of the Course

The course's concluding phase accentuates the amplification of cognitive presence: amalgamated presentation, personal advancement, introspection, and assessment. Cognitive presence employs the Practical Inquiry (PI) model, rooted in Dewey's reflective thinking notion, encompassing the four stages of triggering events: exploration, amalgamation, and resolution. This juncture of the blended course is pivotal in determining students' aptitude to achieve elevated objectives and nurture their capabilities. Though learners exhibit pronounced learning motivation during the initial triggering and exploratory

Table 2. A Typical Example of Mid-Course Blended Learning Activity Design

Activities	Strategies	Style
Project design	Promote individual and group knowledge building	Online/offline
Face-to-face instruction	Motivate students to stay engaged	Offline
Project implementation	Motivate students to stay engaged	Offline
Brainstorm	Promote individual and group knowledge building	Offline
Project summary	Guide students to learn effectively	Offline
Wonderful sharing	Motivate students to stay engaged	Online/offline
members assessment	Motivate students to stay engaged	Offline

phases, this enthusiasm wanes as learning complexity escalates, often preventing students from advancing to the integration and resolution phases. Consequently, teachers should prioritize high-level cognitive presence "solution" activities, offering resolutions to students' challenges. This ensures that students seamlessly navigate the PI model's stages, translating and applying acquired knowledge to real-world quandaries and fostering self-growth and introspection through comprehensive performance display tasks.

For instance, in the higher vocational elective course "Traditional Chinese Colors," the project-oriented concluding phase (post-course 4 weeks) can incorporate the subsequent blended learning activities (listed as Table 3): This course's final phase emphasizes knowledge application and transfer from the preliminary conceptual phase. Teachers present reference materials and exemplars, aiding students in addressing analogous issues. Learners, leveraging the online platform's resources, tackle problems under direct, in-person teacher guidance, creating various artworks for juxtaposition and self-assessment to select the paramount design. Upon online submission, peer discussions and evaluations ensue, followed by teacher grading and public commendations. Apart from online feedback, teachers curate result-centric aesthetic exhibitions in offline settings. Through schoolwide peer evaluations, group cross-assessments, and self-assessments, students deeply introspect and consolidate, bolstering problem-solving and self-reflection proficiencies. The explicit objective of showcasing the final "Traditional Chinese Colors" work propels students to explore, amalgamate, and translate aesthetic education knowledge, culminating in tangible innovative artworks, thus completing both individual and collective knowledge establishment.

Table 3. Typical Examples of End-Course Blended Learning Activity Design

Activities	Strategies	Style
Personal creation	Comprehensive presentation and self-development	Offline
Exhibition of works	Comprehensive presentation and self-development	Online
Social evaluation	Self-reflection and evaluation	Online, offline
Group peer assessment	Self-reflection and evaluation	Online, offline
Self-evaluation	Self-reflection and evaluation	Offline

4 Conclusion

In view of the phenomenon of "pseudo-learning" in blended learning, the existing blended learning focuses too much on the design of teaching resources, but fail to provide effective verification for students' learning outcome. Guided by the Community of Inquiry, this paper studies the design of project-driven blended learning activities for higher vocational general elective courses, which captures the core of blended learning, and teachers should pay attention to different aspects in the periods of blended learning: (1) At the beginning of the course, teachers focus on creating social presence. Build a sense of trust and belonging, create a positive learning atmosphere, and encourage group cooperation. (2) In the middle of the course, teachers focus on creating teaching presence. Guide students to learn effectively, promote individual and group knowledge gaining, and motivate students to participate the task. (3) At the end of the course, teachers should strengthen cognitive presence, promote comprehensive display and self-development, self-reflection and evaluation. The results show that based on the project-driven blended learning activity in higher vocational general elective courses has a significant role in cultivating students' thinking and abilities in work achievement, learning cognition and interpersonal relationships.

Acknowledgements. The article was funded by Shenzhen Education Sciences Planning Program 'Blended Learning under Public Emergency in Higher Vocational Colleges - Taking General Elective Courses as an Example'. Number: ybfz20015.

References

1. Guoshuai, L.: The community of inquiry theoretical model: a research paradigm for online and blended learning. Open Educ. Res. **24**(1), 29–40 (2018)
2. Yan, C.: Exploration on the design of blended learning activities of English interpretation in colleges and universities under the background of "Internet +." Chinese J. ICT Educ. **20**, 62–65 (2018)
3. Xiaoying, F., Yijun, W., Jieting, C., et al.: Designing blended learning activities for the Internet Plus age. Chinese J. Distance Educ. (**06**), 60–67+77 (2021)
4. Xiaoying, F., Jieting, C., Luoying, H.: Designing blended learning in the Internet plus era. Chinese J. Distance Educ. (**08**), 25–32+54+77 (2020)

5. Garrison, D.R., Anderson, T., Archer, W., et al.: The first decade of the community of inquiry framework: a retrospective. Internet and Higher Educ. **13**(1–2), 5–9 (2010)
6. Castellanos-Reyes, D.: 20 years of the community of inquiry framework. TechTrends **64**(4), 557–560 (2020)
7. Archer, W.: Beyond online discussions: Extending the community of inquiry framework to entire courses. Internet High. Educ. **13**(1–2), 69 (2010)
8. Kumar, S., Dawson, K., Black, E.W., et al.: Applying the community of inquiry framework to an online professional practice doctoral program. Int. Rev. Res. Open Distrib. Learn. **12**(6), 126–142 (2011)
9. Akyol, Z., Vaughan, N., Garrison, D.R.: The impact of course duration on the development of a community of inquiry. Interact. Learn. Environ. **19**(3), 231–246 (2011)
10. Cooper, T., Scriven, R.: Communities of inquiry in curriculum approach to online learning: Strengths and limitations in context. Australas. J. Educ. Technol. **33**(4), 22–37 (2017)
11. Lowenthal, P.R., Dunlap, J.C.: Problems measuring social presence in a community of inquiry. E-Learn. Digital Media **11**(1), 19–30 (2014)
12. Garrison, D.R., Cleveland-Innes, M., Fung, T.S.: Exploring causal relationships among teaching, cognitive and social presence: student perceptions of the community of inquiry framework. Internet High. Educ. **13**(1–2), 31–36 (2010)
13. Guo, P., Saab, N., Wu, L., et al.: The Community of Inquiry perspective on students 'social presence, cognitive presence, and academic performance in online project-based learning.' J. Comput. Assist. Learn. **37**(5), 1479–1493 (2021)
14. Lee, K., Fanguy, M.: Online exam proctoring technologies: educational innovation or deterioration? Br. J. Edu. Technol. **53**(3), 475–490 (2022)
15. Berry, S.: Teaching to connect: Community-building strategies for the virtual classroom. Online Learn. **23**(1), 164–183 (2019)

Data Standard Construction

Zhengxuan Duan[✉], Shaolei Zhou, and Zhicheng Wu

Beijing Institute of Beijing Jinghang Research Institute of Computing and Communication, Beijing 100074, China
zhousl1399@163.com

Abstract. Data standardization is a series of work on the definition and implementation of data standards to achieve data value driven business development. The data standard system is a scientific and reasonable framework built according to the actual situation of enterprises, and it is the basis for data standardization. The formulation of data standards requires the investigation of the current situation of data standards, in-depth understanding of the current data problems and the understanding and expectations of various business departments on data standards. Determine the design ideas and relevant principles of data standards. When implementing data standards, we need to consider the implementation strategies and schemes of data standards, and analyze the mapping and differences of data standards. The implementation of data standards needs to consider the implementation of business level and system level.

Keywords: Data standards · Standard formulation · Standard landing · Data

1 Introduction

Data is a fundamental support element for the army's business development, and high-quality data is a necessary condition for improving business efficiency and strengthening management and analysis capabilities, and data standardization is a key foundational work for improving data quality. Through data standardization, data will be turned into resources [1, 2], and through the processing and analysis of data, it will provide support for the development of the army, precipitate data assets, and give play to the value of data. Therefore, data standardization is an important cornerstone of data management and application.

The value of data standardization is reflected on the one hand in promoting communication in various fields and laying a good foundation for information construction, and on the other hand, it lies in meeting the requirements of regulatory authorities for data. Data standardization can help the military achieve the following data values:

(1) Improve the overall efficiency: data standardization unifies the business language, clarifies the business rules, and standardizes the business processing, thus improving the overall business efficiency and meeting the requirements of management decisions on information [3].

J. Feng et al. (Eds.): EDGE 2023, LNCS 14205, pp. 46–54, 2024.
https://doi.org/10.1007/978-3-031-51826-3_5

(2) Improve data quality: data standardization unifies the data definitions of various systems, so data standardization will directly improve the quality of data, providing accurate and comprehensive data for the leadership's management decisions [3].

(3) Enhance IT implementation capability: Data standardization will enhance the data model design efficiency of IT systems, reduce the complexity of integration between various systems, and provide consistent data definitions for various business lines and IT systems, thus facilitating interactions between various business lines, reducing the complexity of data exchange between various systems, and enhancing the ability to share data, which in turn lays the foundation for enhancing IT implementation capability [3].

2 Relationship of Data Standards to Various Domains

Data standards are one of the components of data management activities, complementing data governance and data application. Data standard work needs to be carried out in line with the focus of the work, supporting the establishment of relevant management mechanisms for data standards, using data standards as a breakthrough for data governance work, improving data quality, providing basic data support for data applications and services, and promoting the contribution of data management to business, management and science and technology.

The relationship between data standard management and each field is described below:

(1) Relationship with data value creation: data value creation provides the construction of data standard management with unified data management focus and goals at the enterprise-wide level, and practical application of data value, quantitative analysis application, decision support, and risk identification.

(2) Relationship with data management organizations and responsibilities: data management organizations and responsibilities define the data standard management role system, organizational structure and division of responsibilities, providing an organizational basis for the development of data standard management work.

(3) Relationship with the data management system: the data management system regulates the objectives of the data standards management area, the action guidelines to follow, the clear tasks to be accomplished, the actual way of working, the general steps to be taken and specific measures.

(4) Relationship with data architecture and model: data architecture and model management as an important carrier of data standards, along with the adjustment or change of data standards data architecture and model will also do the corresponding adjustment and optimization;

(5) Relationship with data quality: data standard management provides technical standards and business standards for data quality management, and serves as the basis for the formulation of data quality measurement rules, which helps to improve data quality; at the same time, data standard improvement or change requirements are put forward due to the optimization of business processes or change of information items in the process of data quality improvement management;

(6) Relationship with metadata: business data standards are the data source of meta-data management module, while technical data standards serve as the comparison standard for technical metadata;

(7) Relationship with master data: master data management clarifies the business defini-tion and technical definition of master data, which makes the business and technical departments have the same understanding of master data and standardizes the defi-nition of master data in the construction of each system. The formulation of master data standards can be combined with the existing data standards as a reference; at the same time, changes in the business and technical definitions of master data are also used as inputs for the definition of data standards.

3 Data Standard Development

The data standardization work is divided into three stages: status quo research, standard design and standard release.

3.1 Current Research on Data Standards

3.1.1 Objectives of Data Standard Status Quo Research

The goal of the status quo research stage is to gain an in-depth understanding of the current data problems and the business sector's understanding and expectations of the data standards through different forms of research, and to verify and analyze the causes of the problems from different levels. Specific objectives include:

(1) From the business level, business interviews are researched to provide input for subsequent access to data standards and business definitions of information items.

(2) From the system level, through the query and comparison of system data dictionary, it provides the basis for the harmonization of data standard information items across systems and the technical definition of information items.

(3) From the statistical and external regulatory level, the analysis of business interviews and information provided by business units provides the basis for the development of data standard information item codes to ensure that the necessary information is available to meet the demands of increasingly sophisticated statistical and regulatory reporting.

(4) From the management level, business interviews and analysis of organizational func-tions are used to lay the foundation for the design, maintenance, and management of subsequent data standards.

3.1.2 Research Methods on the Status of Data Standards

Aiming at the business characteristics of the data standards of each theme, combined with the practical experience of similar projects in the past, the research content is mainly carried out from the following aspects:

(1) Business Interviews

Through interviews with relevant business departments and sub-centers, the role of each theme data in business development and current system support is under-stood. The status quo of each theme data is grasped at the business level, and the understanding and knowledge of the business departments on the work content of data standards is strengthened, which is conducive to the cooperation of the two sides' work.

(2) Data Analysis

By organizing and analyzing the collected information, including the current system information as well as the systems and reports collected from various business departments, the project team will have a more complete and accurate understanding of the current status of the data on various topics.

(3) System Research

In response to the business problems identified, we understand and verify the relevant attributes of the data that cause business problems at the system level and analyze the causes through data dictionary inquiries. Meanwhile, for specific systems or projects, we communicate with relevant technical personnel to gain a deeper understanding of the relevant processes and rules of specific systems in dealing with information on various topics, and to understand the existing data problems and potential needs.

3.2   Design Ideas and Related Principles of Data Standard

3.2.1   Principles for the Preparation of Data Standards

The data standard framework in general focuses on the scientific and rational nature of the standard system framework for standard classification. Considering the actual needs of informatization and business development on the data standards put forward by the continuous updating, expansion and extension of the requirements, but also pay attention to the existing international, national and military standards of mutual convergence. The data standard system needs to follow the principles of practicality, foresight and openness in its preparation.

(1) Practicality: The data standard system must meet the practical needs of the development of various tasks and specific data applications, reflecting the characteristics and highlighting the key points. The definition of data standards and the implementation of operational and technical level data standards are in accordance with the data standards landing implementation program.

(2) Forward-looking. Actively draw on international experience and make full reference to the advanced practical experience of the industry at home and abroad, our army and foreign armies, so that the data standard system can fully reflect the development direction of the business.

(3) Openness: The standards contained in the data standards system should be revisable and enforceable, not static. The entire standard system should be continuously enriched and updated with business development and in-depth application of data standards. The data standards system should be expandable.

3.2.2   Principles of Access to Data Standards

For data standards, the focus is the data that is used and exchanged with high frequency within the organization. It is not necessary to include all data in the scope of data standards. So the following access principles for the scope of data standards are established from the point of view of the guiding role of data standards for business and IT [4].

Principle 1: Data standards that have been officially issued by international, national or military organizations, data specifications that have been explicitly requested by other formal organizations and data specifications that have been clarified in a document issued by the unit can be included in the data standards system.

Principle 2: Data and codes that are widely used across the organization, especially across lines of business, can be standardized [5].

Principle 3: Data and code used in multiple places in existing IT systems can be standardized.

Principle 4: For analytical indicators, Standardization should only be carried out for aggregated analytical indicators, while analytical indicators used in individual business areas will not be included in the scope of standardization for the time being.

4   Data Standards Implementation

Data standards implementation is divided into three phases: data standards implementation proposal design, data standards mapping and variance analysis, and data standards implementation.

4.1   Proposal Design for Implementation of Data Standards

4.1.1   Strategy for the Implementationof Data Standards

The implementation of data standards is a continuous work, and its value is indisputable. However, in the process of implementation, it will also bring the workload and complexity of transformation to system construction. How to balance the inputs and outputs of the phases so as to maximize the marginal benefits is the primary principle of data standards implementation, and its key elements include:

(1) Difficulty of system modification and risk consideration
   a. Minimize the transformation cost of the operational system already in production and the risk of additional problems.
   b. Consider the feasibility of outsourcing mature software system transformation.
   c. For system implementation projects, data standards are implemented as far as possible without extending the project implementation cycle.
(2) The way of implementation
   a. The transformation of the source system is the most direct way to implement data standards, which helps to control the quality of future data entry.
   b. The transformation of the interface between systems is an important work to ensure the consistency of interaction.
   c. The data will be transformed according to the standard when the data enter the data warehouse, which can guarantee the accuracy of statistical analysis.
(3) Prioritization of business value realization
   a. Prioritize the implementation of data standards by analyzing the benefits of business operations and management.
   b. Prioritization of data standard implementation is ranked through gain analysis of business statistical analysis and regulatory reporting.

c. For data standards content of high relevance, it is recommended to implement the landing at the same time.

(4) Overall IT planning arrangements

The implementation of data standards should be in accordance with the overall arrangement of IT planning construction steps rhythmically and systematically.

The implementation of data standards requires the following strategies:

(1) Issue-driven: Based on the requirements for the consistency of important industry codes, organization information and product information in risk management, regulatory reporting and statistical analysis, the implementation of corresponding data standards will be carried out with the aim of solving the most urgent data problems of the business departments as the starting point for the implementation of data standards.

(2) Driven by business refinement management: Based on the content of data standards, analyze the role of corresponding data items (customer information, asset information, product characteristic information, etc.) in enhancing business management refinement to ensure that the business value of data standards can be quickly reflected, and then promote the implementation of corresponding data standards.

(3) Data consistency drive: Seize the opportunity of reconstructing important IT systems to promote the implementation of data standards, while simultaneously advocating for data standardization in related IT systems. Ultimately, this will ensure the full implementation of data standards and guarantee consistency in data definitions.

4.1.2 Principles for the Implementation of Data Standards

The following principles should govern the binding of the data standards to the various business areas and IT systems when they are implemented:

(1) All business areas and IT systems must follow the standardization of data standards, requiring the mandatory implementation of business standards, technical standards and code standards for information items. In addition, the quasi-standard needs to be implemented as a recommended standard for reference in business areas and IT systems.

(2) The standardized data model is used only as a reference and is not required to be enforced. On the one hand, the reference data model defined by the data standard does not cover all data items, and on the other hand, it takes into account the different individual needs of each business area and IT system.

(3) For newly built or revamped systems, it is mandatory to implement the business standards, technical standards and code standards for information items. For existing systems, when their data enter the data platform (mainly referring to the data warehouse), they must follow the business standards, technical standards and code standards of information items for conversion to ensure the consistency of subsequent statistical analysis.

4.2 Mapping and Variance Analysis of Data Standards

Data standards mapping and discrepancy analysis is to identify the differences between data standards and source system data dictionaries, and to establish data mapping relationships between data standards and source systems. Based on the completely defined data standard templates, the data mapping and discrepancy analysis work of key systems is the basis for subsequent data quality analysis and the development of systematic data cleansing and quality improvement programs. The analysis of data standard discrepancy analysis mainly includes the following aspects:

(1) Whether data items are accessible from the source system or data warehouse;
(2) Whether the content of the data is consistent across different systems;
(3) Which data currently need to be obtained through the data warehouse, which of them have been entered into the data warehouse, and which data have not been entered into the data warehouse;
(4) In-depth analysis of the reasons for the differences between the systems and the data standard templates.

The data standard discrepancy analysis is carried out for the data warehouse and the data discrepancy of each source system. Data discrepancy analysis is not just a simple comparison of the data items of the data standard template with the data mapping results, but a scientific and rigorous in-depth analysis of the relevant data items in each system based on the complete definition of the data standard template, the specific work steps are as follows:

Step 1: Collect, organize, and understand the data dictionary of the data warehouse and each source system, as well as the interrelationships between the data, in order to prepare for data standard mapping and disparity analysis.

Step 2: Reasonably arrange the order of data discrepancy analysis work and promote data discrepancy analysis in phases to ensure that the results of data discrepancy analysis are prudent and correct, and to lay the foundation for the subsequent data quality analysis work.

Step 3: Conduct multiple interviews with technical staff of the data warehouse and each source system to gain a detailed understanding of the current status of the data warehouse and the source system, the system transformation plan and the system upgrade plan, and carefully analyze the extent to which the existing system and data support each data item in the data standard template.

Step 4: The data standards discrepancy analysis work is carried out by project team members in cooperation with technical members who have experience in implementing business systems and data warehouses, because the technical members have a deep understanding of both the target data and the actual data involved in the data standards discrepancy analysis.

Step 5: After fully considering the business process requirements, internal management needs, and the actual situation of the existing system and data architecture, first carry out the data standard mapping and data discrepancy analysis of the data warehouse. Mainly analyze the following:

(1) Determine whether the data item exists in the data warehouse and whether it needs to be mapped from the data source system data;
(2) Data warehouse table names and field names;
(3) Mapping logic, data fetching and conversion rules, and description of differences.

Step 6: Based on the data mapping results of the data warehouse, for the data items that cannot be obtained from the data warehouse, carry out data mapping and discrepancy analysis of the source system, mainly analyzing the following:

(4) Whether the data item exists in the source system;
(5) Source system table names;
(6) Source system table names and field names;
(7) Mapping logic, data fetching and conversion rules, and description of differences.

Step 7: The technical members involved in the data mapping and discrepancy analysis work will also make direct use of the results of the data mapping in the data quality diagnosis and data standards and inspection rules development phases to carry out quality analysis and formulate quality inspection rules, so as to maximize the use of the experience gained from the data mapping and discrepancy analysis work.

4.3 Implementation of Data Standards

Data standards implementation consists of both business-level and system-level components.

4.3.1 Implementation Recommendations at the Operational Level

(1) Business system level
        When formulating and revising the business management system, the business management department should incorporate the control and implementation mechanism of data standards at the business level into the business system.
(2) Business operation level
        Integrate data standards into the business operation process, standardize the operation of business operators, follow the requirements of data standards for key data during data entry, and control data quality from the source. At the same time, strengthen the data quality audit in the business operation process, strengthen the review and examination of key data entry, and embed the data control into the business operation process. [6]
(3) Business management and analysis level
        Strengthen the use and implementation of the standard codes and indicators in the data standards for business statistical analysis to ensure the quality of business statistical analysis data and the consistency of the caliber.

4.3.2 Implementation Recommendations at the System Level

(1) New business application system
        In terms of business requirements, integrate the requirements of data standards into the business requirements of the system, and promote the implementation of

data standards in the system with business requirements. In terms of design review and on-line review, focus on reviewing the data model and data interface design of the new system to ensure that data standards are effectively implemented into the system.

(2) Existing business application systems

Comprehensively assess the difficulty, workload and impact on business of implementing data standards in light of the current state of the system, and comprehensively consider the content and implementation path of implementing data standards. Take system transformation as an opportunity and system transformation needs as a focus point to promote the implementation of data standards in existing systems.

5 Conclusion

Data standardization can help enterprises improve data quality, the overall efficiency of business operations and improve IT implementation capabilities. In this article, we focus on the relationship between data standards and other areas, data standards development and data standards implementation. In the development of data standards, it is first necessary to carry out research on the current status of data standards from the business level, the system level, the statistical and external regulatory level, the management level, etc. And then based on the principles of practicality, foresight and openness to the preparation of data standards. Ultimately, based on the principle of access to determine the scope of data to be included in the data standards. In the implementation of data standards, it is necessary to determine the data standards implementation program and carry out mapping and discrepancy analysis of data standards with reference to the program to guide the implementation of data standards.

References

1. Yan, L.: Preliminary practice of data standard system construction of Tianjin port group. Port Sci. Technol. (03), 40–43 (2019)
2. Gu, Q.: Small and medium-sized bank data governance research. SouthWest University of Finance and Economics (2022)
3. Lu, D.: Research on the Construction of a Bank's Data Management System. Shanghai Jiao Tong University, Shanghai (2017)
4. An, X., Wang, Q., Qin, Y., Liang, X.: Promoting the construction of financial standardization to enhance the competitiveness of China's banking Industry. In: Proceedings of the 16th China Standardization Forum, pp. 819–830 (2019)
5. Wei, Z.: Research on Data quality Management of H Bank. Heilongjiang: Harbin Institute of Technology (2014)
6. Wang, M.: Application Research of Financial Control based on ERP System. Shaanxi Normal University, Shaanxi (2015)

Construction and Application of Enterprise Data Assets Based on Data Label System

Lin Liu[1]([⊠]) and Jian Song[2]

[1] Data Governance Senior Manager, Internet Industry, Beijing, China
11328062201@126.com
[2] Data Governance Intermediate Manager, Internet Industry, Beijing, China

Abstract. In the process of enterprise digital transformation, it is hoped that data will play a driving role in the development of new industrial forms and business models. It is required that the data generated from business activities will eventually be empowered into business activities. During this period, data needs to undergo a transformation from resources to assets. In this article, we propose the theory of "data asset growth flywheel" by analyzing the positioning of data assets in enterprises. Then, we demonstrate the precipitation form of enterprise data assets based on its characteristics. Finally, based on the idea that data application should focus on the value scene of business, we provide the methods for enterprises to build and use data assets by developing the data label system.

Keywords: Digital Transformation · Data Assets · Growth Flywheel · Data Label

1 Introduction

With the development of digitalization, data has become an important foundation for enterprises to continuously innovate and create value. It is also an important support for enterprises to develop new industrial forms and business models. The construction and application of data assets is not only a necessary means for enterprises to respond to market changes, but also a key way to achieve digital transformation. In China, the concept and practice of data assets are evolving rapidly, and the country has issued a series of policies to provide guidance and support for the construction and application of enterprise data assets.

In April 2020, the CPC Central Committee and State Council issued the "Opinions on Building a More Perfect Market Based Allocation System and Mechanism for Factors" [1], officially proposing data as the fifth production factor. In 2022, the "14th Five-Year Plan for Digital Economy Development" was released [2], proposing that "it is necessary to focus on high-quality data factors." In December 2022, the CPC Central Committee and State Council issued the "Opinions on Building a Data Basic System to Better Play the Role of Data Factors" [3], known as the "Twenty Points of Data", which has become the top-level design guidance for the construction of China's data factor industry. In order to focus on implementation, on March 10, 2023, the National Data Bureau was

J. Feng et al. (Eds.): EDGE 2023, LNCS 14205, pp. 55–68, 2024.
https://doi.org/10.1007/978-3-031-51826-3_6

established [4]. On August 21, 2023, the Accounting Department of the Ministry of Finance issued the "Interim Provisions on Accounting Treatment Related to Enterprise Data Resources" [5], and "data into accounting" was officially on the way.

To put it simply, data becomes data resources after standardization, data resources become data assets after pricing, and data assets become data factors after being opened. When enterprises actively plan to participate in the construction of data factor market and form a data ecology with "internal and external circulation", they must complete the road from data to data resources and data resources to data assets, and the last step is particularly crucial.

2   The Positioning of Data Assets in the Enterprise

From the perspective of data architecture evolution, the application of data to business can be divided into two stages.

2.1   Data Statistical Analysis with Data Warehouse as the Core

The need to analyze data almost immediately followed the advent of OLTP [6]. In the 1970s, more and more extraction programs began to appear in enterprises. As part of the "natural evolution architecture", the data distribution became a complex "spider web" style. As a result, architectural design for exported data emerged, which ultimately led to the birth of the concept of "data warehouse" in the 1990s.

From the perspective of data application, the importance of data warehouse mainly has the following two points:

(1) The data warehouse provides a transformation path from original data to exported data by hierarchical system design. Data for management is significantly different from data in production systems. This is not limited to the requirement of data indicators, or the design of business system data structures based on the three-paradigms. In today's big data environment, this conclusion still holds.
(2) The data warehouse provides a transformation path from a business perspective to a data perspective by dimensional system design. The data warehouse well connects the indicators from business perspective and the data from technical perspective through dimensions and cubes. It manages the data indicators, on the other hand, it also standardizes the operations of data. All the data usage requirements from the business perspective are converted into indicators, and then standardized through atomic indicators, derived indicators, derived indicators.

Therefore, the data warehouse well supports managers' needs for data statistical analysis. Through enterprise analysis dashboards composed of data indicators, managers can timely grasp the operation and management status of the enterprise and make relevant decisions.

2.2   Data Intelligent Application with Data Middle Platform as the Core

However, statistical analysis only explores half of the data value. After obtaining the basic information contained in data, managers still need to spend a certain amount of time thinking about the next step Therefore, we need to realize the leap from digitalization to intelligence, and to fully explore the data value.

It is difficult for the data indicator system oriented to the "known" to meet the demands. It is necessary to use the power of algorithms to make the data oriented to the "unknown". This is the conversion between causality and correlation, and it is an upgrade of the data warehouse [7].

The data middle platform provides a convenient way to use data. Through microservices, users can flexibly use enterprise data to achieve intelligent applications. Because of this, the data middle platform is normally upgraded from the data warehouse. Through the data warehouse, various data resources of the enterprise are gathered, standardized; and then through the data middle platform, data resources become data assets due to intelligent applications.

We can call the data generated in the first stage "data resources" and the data generated in the second stage "data assets". There are two differences:

(1) Ease of use: Data assets have a broader application space than data resources and are more convenient to use. The data resources existing in the data warehouse focus on statistical analysis. These data structure is also designed to facilitate operations such as roll-up and drill-down of indicators. As a result, the cost of understanding the data is high, which means the readability and understandability are poor. The data assets existing in the data middle platform can cover almost all data application scenarios, making it easier to understand and more convenient.
(2) Estimated economic benefits: Compared with statistical analysis, data-driven intelligent applications are more likely to bring tangible value, including increasing revenue, reducing costs, improving efficiency, etc. Data assets are widely used in enterprises, and their data value has been verified in application scenarios. Therefore, data assets will perform better in the future data factor market.

In the digital economy, the positioning of data assets in enterprises mainly includes two points:

(1) Touchstone of digital construction: Data assets are the achievements of enterprise digital construction, which can intuitively reflect the effectiveness of data system and data management. The precipitation of data assets also signifies that enterprise data applications have reached a level of "commercialization", which means they can deeply participate in frontline business process optimization and improvement, and play a data-driven role internally.
(2) Stepping stone to data factor market: After solving the internal circulation needs, data assets are an important starting point for enterprises to transform internal experience into industry empowerment and then build an external data ecosystem.

3 Data Assets Growth Flywheel

We have clarified the importance of data assets in the enterprise, so how to achieve the healthy accumulation of data assets? We propose the data assets growth flywheel, as shown in * MERGEFORMAT Fig. 1:

The growth of enterprise data assets is mainly divided into five stages: data assets definition, data assets identification, data assets construction, data assets management,

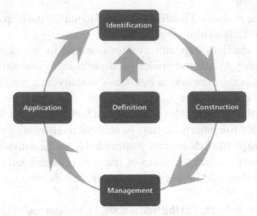

Fig. 1. Data assets growth flywheel

and data assets application, among which construction and application are particularly important.

3.1 Data Assets Definition

Enterprises need to localize their data assets with reference to authoritative sources based on their actual circumstances. The following are currently available for reference:

(1) The "GB/T 40685–2021 Information Technology Service Data Asset Management Requirements" [8] issued by the State Administration for Market Regulation and the China National Standardization Administration defines data assets as "legally owned or controlled data resources that can be measured and bring economic and social value to organizations."

(2) The China Communications Standards Association (CCSA) defines data assets in the "Data Asset Management Practice White Paper (V6.0)" [9] as: "Legally owned or controlled data resources, recorded electronically or otherwise, such as text, images, voice, videos, web pages, databases, sensing signals, can be measured or traded, and can directly or indirectly bring economic and social benefits."

(3) In December 2019, the China Asset Appraisal Association issued the "Expert Guidelines for Asset Appraisal No. 9- Data Asset Appraisal" [10], which defines data assets as "data resources that are legally owned or controlled by a specific entity, can continue to play a role, and can bring direct or indirect economic benefits." Subsequently, in the "Guidelines for Data Asset Appraisal (Draft for Soliciting Opinions)" [11] in June 2022, Revise the definition of data assets to "data resources that are legally owned or controlled by a specific entity, can be measured in monetary terms, and can bring direct or indirect economic benefits."

There are three views on the definition of assets, namely the resource view, the future economic benefit view, and the power view [12]. What the three views have in common is that one emphasizes the past which means legally owned or controlled due to past transactions or events; the second emphasizes the future which means expected to bring economic benefits. The data asset concept can be defined, which should contain at least the following four elements: formed by the past transactions or events, owned or controlled by the enterprise, expected to bring economic benefits to the enterprise, capable of measurement or monetary measurement.

In addition, enterprises can also impose additional constraints on the definition of data assets based on their own data management requirements, such as data scope, data type, degree of control, etc., but the above four elements should be the "minimum set" that must be included.

3.2 Data Assets Identification

By definition, data assets cannot be well identified, so we need to further summarize the key characteristics of data assets and use them to accurately identify data assets.

(1) Clear data rights based on the past: The "Twenty Points of Data" divides data rights into the right to hold, the right to use, and the right to operate. One of the key characteristics of data assets is to ensure the clarity of the above three rights through legal or agreement constraints.
(2) Reliable quality based on the past: Data assets must be built by processed and high qualified data. The higher the quality of data, the higher its utilization rate, and correspondingly, the easier it is to generate economic value.
(3) Ease of use based on the future: ease of use directly affects whether the data will eventually become an "asset" or a "contingent asset". Data is valuable when it is easy to use. The ease of use of data assets is measured from the three levels of ease of reading, ease of understanding, and ease of using [14], and quantitative scoring standards are constructed through the analytic hierarchy process and the expert method to evaluate the ease of use.
(4) Estimated value based on the future: Whether it is facing data-driven business applications within the enterprise or facing the construction of a data-enabled ecosystem outside the enterprise, quantitative assessment of data assets value is essential. It should be noted that different methods (such as cost method, income method, and market method) should be used to evaluate the value of data assets in different scenarios.

3.3 Data Assets Construction

When enterprises carry out data assets construction, they usually form a series of data carriers such as data models, data indicators, data labels, API interface services, etc. Different precipitation methods correspond to different constructions, but in summary, they can be divided into the followings:

(1) Data finding: According to the characteristics of data assets, sort out various data resources of the enterprise and find qualified data resources as the key target. The metadata information of data resources should be collected and organized from data perspective, business perspective, and technical perspective.
(2) Data integration: Enterprises have different data sources. Whether it is heterogeneity between various systems or differences in internal and external data environments,

it will bring about the problem of inconsistency in similar data. Therefore, data integration needs to be carried out from a unified perspective. Here, we tend to integrate data according to entities Integrating data from different sources according to entities mainly involves two parts of work: First, entity normalization, which means normalizing different entities from different data sources according to unified standards. The second is feature alignment, which involves performing feature disambiguation, feature mapping, and feature completion for different field attributes of the same entity.

(3) Framework building: From the three levels of country, industry, and enterprise, the structured design of the data asset framework needs to meet the following three principles: First, standardization, which means actively citing national and industry standards, and extensively referring to the industry best practices. The second is robustness, which means ensuring the structural robustness and authority of the framework, as well as its stability within a specific scope and time interval. The third is scalability. On the basis of robustness, the framework should allow flexible expansion in response to the development and changes of the business environment.

(4) Content filling: Use appropriate data asset precipitation forms to build enterprise data assets. Different precipitation forms have their own advantages and disadvantages, which will be described in detail in Chapter 4. Through the analysis, combined with the development situation and data management requirement, we can choose the appropriate data precipitation form to meet the needs of business.

3.4 Data Assets Management

Data assets management needs to be carried out based on the four major characteristics of data assets, namely the construction of a security system with clear data rights, the construction of a governance system with reliable data quality, the construction of a service system with ease of use, and the construction of an operation system with estimable value.

(1) Construction of a security system with clear data rights: The rights to hold and operate data can usually only be clarified and restricted by legal agreements. However, the right to use data requires further refinement and improvement of the data security system, including the right to query, the right to modify, the right to delete, etc.

(2) Construction of a governance system with reliable data quality: With the goal of ultimately improving data quality, data assets are managed according to the DAMA system [15].

(3) Construction of a service system with ease of use: Convenience of use is an important feature of data assets, which will directly affect whether the data can bring expected economic benefits to the enterprise. Traditional methods tend to process data into data products, data services, and even data analysis reports to solve the problem of data servitization. But now, with the evolution of AIGC, intelligent conversational self-service data analysis tools will become a mainstream trend in the future. This is also the way to move towards "data democratization".

(4) Construction of an operation system with estimable value: From an operational perspective, we emphasize improving the circulation mechanism and clearly seeing the value of data. While ensuring the convenience of use, the data circulation situation

can be tracked and analyzed in a timely manner. On this basis, select a data asset evaluation method that is suitable for the enterprise's situation and quantitatively evaluate the value of the data assets.

3.5 Data Assets Application

The application of data assets needs to open up the internal circulation between the data and business, as well as the external circulation between the enterprise and data factor market, as follows:

(1) Internal circulation: Realize the loop between business and digitization, that is, promptly aggregate and organize the data generated in business processes to form enterprise data assets, and then deeply empower the business processes. Through the internal application of data assets, the level of enterprise intelligence is improved, labor operation costs are reduced, and the digital transformation of enterprises is accelerated.

(2) External circulation: Through data assets, enterprises can participate in the construction of the data factor market and build a healthy data ecosystem. On the one hand, enterprises carry out trusted openness of data assets based on security compliance, and then gradually participate in building a prosperous data factor market necessary for production; on the other hand, they seek the data needed for their own development from the data factor market. Data is purchased into the enterprise to accelerate the upgrading and optimization of business processes.

Carrying out data assets applications will further increase the channels for enterprises to obtain data and improve the living environment of data in enterprises. This enables the work on data assets to eventually form a benign growth flywheel, completing the closed loop of data assets from definition, to identification, to construction, to management, and finally to application.

4 Selection of Data Asset Precipitation Form

Data comes in a variety of forms, including files, data models, data indicators, data labels, API interface services, etc. When carrying out data asset construction, it is necessary to complete the selection of data asset precipitation form in a single or combined manner according to the company's own needs.

4.1 Analysis of Several Precipitation Forms

Several common forms of data precipitation are shown below.

(1) Data model. Using data model as the precipitation form of data assets is the most common method in enterprises. The advantage of data model is that it is easy to carry out data quality management. But the problems are also obvious. Firstly, the convenience of use is poor. Business personnel need to know how to operate the database and have the ability to write SQL. The second is the usage permission

control. Due to the design of the database, it cannot be easily achieved at the row-column level. This will lead to situations where permission management is out of control, such as data leakage.

(2) Data indicator: When managers begin to use dashboards and reports to analyze and make decisions on commercial and operational activities, a large number of data indicators will be generated. Data indicator has the advantage of better readability, and the permission management and value assessment of data assets have been upgraded to the system level to meet the needs of refinement. However, there are three main shortcomings of this method. Firstly, the management of data quality is relatively complicated. Secondly, although the indicators are readable, it still takes a certain amount of effort to completely understand the meaning of the indicators. Thirdly, the usage scenarios are limited to data analysis operations in statistical dimensions, and cannot cope with the uncertain data mining in a big data environment.

(3) Data label: Using data label as a form of precipitation of data assets has become popular in recent years. Compared with data indicators, the application scenarios of data labels are closer to the business processes, such as customer acquisition, potential mining, retaining, transforming, etc. Therefore, it will be more convenient and clearer when measuring the value of data assets. In addition, the advantage of data labels is that they are easy to read and understand. The only drawback is that its data quality control, like data indicators, has complex logic and long troubleshooting cycles.

(4) API interface service: Using API interface service as the precipitation form of data assets is a method oriented to business production activities, which pays more attention to the real-time requirements of the business system for data usage. The advantage of this method is that it is supported by the system in terms of rights management and value evaluation. The disadvantage is that the readability and understandability are relatively weak.

When choosing the form of data asset deposition, Table 1 can help to analyze advantages and disadvantages of the different precipitation forms mentioned above.

Table 1. Comparison table of data asset precipitation forms (sample)

	Clarity of data permissions	Reliable quality	Easy to read	Easy to understand	Easy to use	Value estimable
Data Model	★★	★★★	★	★	★★	★★
Data Indictor	★★★	★★	★★★	★★	★★	★★★
Data Label	★★★	★★	★★★	★★★	★★★	★★★
API Interface	★★★	★★	★★	★★	★★★	★★★

4.2 Reason of Choosing the Data Label System

Among the above forms of data asset accumulation, we are more inclined to choose the data label. Reasons are following:

(1) Excellent ease of use: An important feature of data assets is ease of use, which makes it possible to generate expected economic benefits in the future. Firstly, it uses entities as the core perspective, and various attributes and behavioral information of entities are classified and marked to facilitate data integration and unified management. Secondly, users can quickly locate target data through simple query and filter. Thirdly, the data label system ensures flexibility and scalability.
(2) The possibility of being deeply embedded in business processes: Data is an abstraction from the physical world to the digital world. The abstraction process includes conceptual model design, logical model design and physical model design. The data label system is a concrete representation of data from the digital world to the physical world. It can clearly express the entities, the attributes, and the relationships between them in the physical world. This kind of data expression not only facilitates business personnel to understand the data, but also increases the possibility of deeply embedding it into business processes.
(3) Outstanding inclusiveness: From the perspective of content, data labels can be divided into three categories: the first category is descriptive labels, which objectively describe the information in the logistics world. The second category is statistical labels, which are used to realize data statistics of different dimensions through mathematical calculations. The third category is predictive tags, which are used to predict and analyze potential trends and future directions through data mining, machine learning, etc. Therefore, the data label system can cover data content in different forms such as data models, data indicators, API services, etc.
(4) More intuitive value expression: Compared with back-end scenarios such as data indicators and data analysis for decision support, data label system is usually directly involved in front-line business processes. Therefore, it will be easier to form a data-driven value closed-loop, and help enterprises to create new industries and new business formats.

5 Data Label System Construction

As mentioned above, the construction of the data label system is divided into four parts: data finding, data integration, framework building, and content filling.

5.1 Data Finding

We inventory available data resources from both inside and outside the enterprise.

From an internal perspective of an enterprise, business activities will generate a large amount of data. Generally, they come from Business system, database, Data warehouse, data lake, Log information and Unstructured files.

From an external perspective of the enterprise, through data procurement and other forms, the enterprise obtain data for its own development in accordance with the law and regulations, mainly including Macro policy environment data, Mesomarket industry data and Micro capability service data.

5.2 Data Integration

Data integration mainly includes the following two aspects:

(1) Data preprocessing: Develop unified standards for data labels, including data factor standards, data structure standards, reference data standards, etc., and uniformly clean data from different data sources based on the standards. The cleaning process mainly includes outlier processing, missing value completion, standard value conversion, etc.
(2) Data combination: Preprocessed data sets from different sources are integrated through algorithmic techniques such as probability theory, evidence theory, fuzzy sets, and neural networks. The integration includes two parts. Firstly, entity unification, which disambiguates and correlates data related to the same entity or different data sources. Secondly, feature alignment, which aligns the description features of the same entity from different data sources, including disambiguation, mapping, completion and other work.

5.3 Framework Building

The data label system includes three aspects: label objects, label categories, and data labels. The overall framework diagram is shown in Fig. 2:

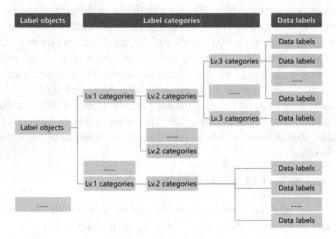

Fig. 2. Overall framework diagram of data label system

In the diagram:

(1) Digital mapping can attribute everything in the real world to objects. Based on business scenarios and actual process conditions, objects can be divided into three major types: "people", "things" and "relationships". In the construction of the data label system, label objects are usually entities of enterprise concerned, such as employees, customers, suppliers, orders, contracts, products, after-sales services, etc.

(2) The label category is a tree structure distributed under the root directory label object. The first-level branch that grows from the root directory label object is called the first-level category, the second-level branch that grows from the first-level branch is called the second-level category, and so on. Category level is up to three, and data labels can be mounted on categories except the first-level category. The advantage is that the category structure is relatively clear, making it easier for subsequent users to browse and use.

(3) A label category contains at least one data label, and usually takes into account standardization and ease of use, with no more than 50 at most. In addition, the same data label can only be mounted to one label category and cannot be mounted repeatedly.

5.4 Content Filling

The core of building a data label system is to focus on entities and carry out category construction and label construction.

In the construction of content level, the following three aspects need to be considered:

(1) Build a data integration system around entities. Identify entities and virtual entities involved in enterprise business processes from the three perspectives of people, objects, and relationships, and integrate data from different sources, formats, and structures to form a unified and comprehensive view of data.

(2) Refining data service capabilities based on categories. Subdividing and classifying data labels through the label category system can improve the accuracy of data service capabilities, thereby helping users make better use of data.

(3) Use labels to realize the value of data assets. Maximize the value of data assets through the in-depth use of data labels in business processes.

Regarding the selection of entity objects, sorting out the entities and virtual entities involved in the enterprise's business processes from the three perspectives of people, objects, and relationships.

Regarding the design of label categories, the "research induction method" can be used. Summarize the common characteristics from some individual or special cases of the survey situation, and then derive general conclusions. Details are as follows:

(1) Research: We investigate the overall framework and business activities at the national level, industry level, and enterprise level respectively in two dimensions, theory and practice.

(2) Induction: We use complete induction or incomplete induction to organize the data and classification information obtained from the survey, and finally merge them to form a standardized, authoritative, and complete label category.

Regarding the development of data labels, it is carried out from three perspectives: descriptive, statistical and predictive, which requires the development of metadata standards for data labels, as well as daily management process specifications for data labels.

6   Label System Application

Around data asset application, we provide product capabilities from data integration, label production, group services, group analysis and insights, group applications and services, and build a data label management platform to empower businesses to complete refined marketing and in-depth operations, and also achieve intelligent growth in data-driven operations. The core functions of the data label management platform are divided into two parts, label development and label application, as shown in Fig. 3.

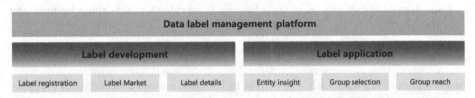

Fig. 3. Core function diagram of data label management platform

The label development part mainly provides the following functions:

(1) Label registration: The platform provides the function of connecting to data sources, and users can use SQL or custom rules to create labels. The metadata configuration function is provided to supplement and improve the metadata information of the labels. Similarly, the platform supports functions such as entity construction and category setting, and finally mounts the configured data labels to the corresponding categories.
(2) Label Market: It usually used as the homepage of the platform, which displays a list of all labels under a certain entity and provides multiple dimensional filtering methods, such as through primary and secondary categories, data sources, application scenarios, usage rights, etc.
(3) Label details: Label details show various metadata information of the label, such as basic information, data information, label identification, usage form, label value score, historical data coverage distribution, label reference details, etc.

The label application part mainly provides the following functions:

(1) Entity Insight: The platform provides functions such as entity portraits, full life cycle analysis, and individual analysis to help users quickly understand the basic attributes and characteristics of entities described by data labels.
(2) Group selection: The platform provides label selection, SQL selection, database table selection and other functions.
(3) Group reach: The platform provides functions such as group management, application reach, and data reach.

Taking individual customers as an example, in terms of entity insights, first of all, customer portraits can be constructed by analyzing data such as customer behavior, interests, and preferences. Secondly, it can help companies understand the life cycle of customers, such as new customers, active customers, lost customers, etc. This can serve as the basis for enterprises to provide personalized recommendations, customized services and precision marketing.

In terms of group selection, customers are divided into different groups or market segments by analyzing data such as customer characteristics, behaviors, and preferences. Group selection can help enterprises rationally allocate resources, avoid resource waste and redundancy, and use limited resources on the most valuable customers, thereby improving market effects and return on investment.

In terms of group reach, information can be conveyed to target groups through a variety of channels, including email, social media, push notifications, etc. The selection of these channels can be determined based on customer usage habits, preferences and frequency of contact to maximize reach effects.

Through data labels, companies can more accurately understand key information such as target customers' interests, preferences, and consumption behaviors. Based on this information, companies can conduct precise market positioning and personalized marketing activities, and recommend products or services to potential customers in a targeted manner. This can improve marketing effects, increase customer click-through rates, conversion rates, and purchase intentions, thereby directly increasing sales revenue and realizing a value closed-loop for data applications.

7 Summary

Digital transformation is the must way for enterprises to pursue innovation and development. By introducing advanced digital technologies and data-driven methods, enterprises can optimize business processes, increase efficiency, and improve user experience. However, digital transformation is not only the process of implementing technology, but more importantly, how to fully utilize and play the role of data. With the advent of the big data era, data has become one of the most important assets of enterprises. By mining and applying data and converting it into commercial value, enterprises can form new economic forms and business models, thereby achieving "new growth". The development of data formats has not only given birth to new industries and markets, but also brought more business opportunities and profit growth points to enterprises. The construction and application of enterprise data assets based on the data label is a highly systematic and convenient way. This article comprehensively elaborates on the construction and application of data assets based on the data label in methodology level and practical level, hoping to inspire enterprises to think about data system work in digital transformation.

References

1. Central Committee of the Communist Party of China and the State Council. Opinions on building a more complete system and mechanism for market-oriented allocation of factors [EB/OL]. (2020). 21 Sep 2023. https://www.gov.cn/zhengce/2020-04/09/content_5500622.htm
2. Central committee of the communist party of china and the state council. 14th Five-Year Plan Digital Economy Development Plan [EB/OL] (2022). 21 Sep 2023. https://www.gov.cn/zhengce/content/2022-01/12/content_5667817.htm

3. CPC central committee and state council. Opinions on building a data infrastructure system to better utilize the role of data factors [EB/OL] (2022). 21 Sep 2023. https://www.gov.cn/zhengce/2022-12/19/content_5732695.htm

4. Central committee of the communist party of China and the state council. Reform plan for party and state institutions [EB/OL] (2023). 21 Sep 2023. https://www.gov.cn/gongbao/content/2023/content_5748649.htm

5. Ministry of finance of the People's Republic of China. Interim provisions on accounting treatment related to enterprise data resources [EB/OL] (2023). 21 Sep 2023. https://kjs.mof.gov.cn/zhengcefabu/202308/t20230821_3903354.htm

6. Inmon, W.H.: Building the data warehouse. 4. Wiley 07 Oct 2005

7. Viktor, M.-S.: A Revolution that will transform how we live, work, and think. 1. Eamon Dolan/Houghton Mifflin Harcourt 5 Mar 2013

8. GB/T 40685-2021. Information technology service data asset management requirements. China Standards Press, Beijing (2021)

9. China academy of information and communications technology. Data asset management practice white paper 6.0 [R/OL] (2023). 21 Sep 2023. http://221.179.172.81/images/20230104/12651672818383015.pdf

10. China asset appraisal association. Asset appraisal expert guidelines No. 9 - Data Asset Appraisal [R/OL] (2020). 23 Sep 2021. www.cas.org.cn

11. China assessment association. data asset assessment guidance (Draft for Comment) [EB/OL] (2022). 21 Sep 2023. http://www.cas.org.cn/ggl/6249335e6a73493fb6e6ad854164f07c.htm

12. Nan, J.: Principles of asset valuation (4th edn). 4. Dongbei University of Finance and Economics Press, Liaoning (2018)

13. GB/T 33850-2017. Information technology service quality evaluation index system. China Standards Press, Beijing (2017)

14. Ren, Y.: Tag category system: business-oriented data asset design methodology. 1. Machinery Industry Press, 25 May 2021

15. DAMA international. DAMA Data Management Knowledge System Guide. Tsinghua University Press, Beijing (2016)

Secure and Fast Query Approach for High-Precision Multi-dimensional Satellite Remote Sensing Data

Zhengxiang Cheng[1], Weixuan Mao[1], Ruwang Wen[1], Zhuolin Mei[1,2,3(✉)],
Bin Wu[1,2,3], Jiaoli Shi[1,2,3], and Xiao Cheng[1,2,3]

[1] School of Computer and Big Data Science, Jiujiang University, Jiujiang Jiangxi, China
meizhuolin@126.com
[2] Jiujiang Key Laboratory of Network and Information Security, Jiujiang, Jiangxi, China
[3] Institute of Information Security, Jiujiang University, Jiujiang, Jiangxi, China

Abstract. High-precision satellite remote sensing data provides rich and accurate Earth observation information that can be used for various remote sensing applications. In this era of edge computing with the Internet of Things at its core, network edge devices generate massive amounts of real-time data. However, network edge data, such as remote sensing data, may contain sensitive information. Therefore, ensuring the security of massive remote sensing data while providing fast and secure retrieval has become a challenge. However, many existing solutions only address problems in single-dimensional remote sensing data scenarios, while others are not efficient. Therefore, we propose a secure and fast query approach for high-precision multi-dimensional satellite remote sensing data (SFQA) to address the efficiency and security issues of querying multi-dimensional remote sensing data. In SFQA, we use more efficient encoding techniques to replace the complex and time-consuming encryption algorithms used in traditional methods. Additionally, we construct a secure index to achieve secure and efficient querying of massive high-resolution multi-dimensional satellite remote sensing data. Experimental results and analysis show that the SFQA method performs efficiently in querying high-resolution multi-dimensional satellite remote sensing data. Furthermore, our security analysis confirms that no external entity can access or obtain any additional information throughout the entire query process, ensuring the confidentiality and privacy of remote sensing data.

Keywords: high-precision · remote sensing data · edge computing · multi-dimension · privacy · querying

1 Introduction

In recent years, remote sensing technology has experienced rapid development [1, 2]. Remote sensing technology can be applied to various scenarios, such as geological exploration, environmental monitoring, agriculture management, natural resource management, urban planning, disaster monitoring, and response [3, 4]. Among them, a large

J. Feng et al. (Eds.): EDGE 2023, LNCS 14205, pp. 69–81, 2024.
https://doi.org/10.1007/978-3-031-51826-3_7

amount of remote sensing data needs to be processed and analyzed. Compared with traditional cloud computing, edge computing distributes data processing tasks at the edge of the network, thereby reducing data transmission delay and improving data processing efficiency. However, the collected satellite remote sensing data may contain sensitive information [5, 6]. For example, monitoring data for agricultural crops often includes information such as temperature, light intensity, and soil nutrients 7. Therefore, securely storing the collected high-precision remote sensing data and efficiently extracting specific data from the massive volumes of high-precision remote sensing data is a challenge that needs to be addressed.

Currently, many efficient ciphertext retrieval schemes have been proposed to handle data. The efficient ciphertext retrieval schemes are mainly classified into three classes: order-preserving encryption (OPE), bucketization schemes, and secure index schemes. However, most current OPE schemes [8–11] can only support queries on the ciphertexts of single-dimensional data and rarely consider queries on the ciphertexts of multi-dimensional data 12. In addition, since attackers can accurately infer the corresponding plaintexts from the ordering information of ciphertexts in OPE schemes, there is a serious security issue 13. Bucketization schemes can be used to protect the ordering information of ciphertexts and support queries on the ciphertexts of multi-dimensional data [14–16]. However, in bucketization schemes, the bucket information is stored locally, which is not convenient for data users 14. To further improve the efficiency of bucketization schemes and outsource the bucket information to a third-party server, secure index schemes have been proposed [14–17] However, the basic encryption scheme used in [14–17] is the matrix encryption technique 14, which is not efficient enough.

Considering the limitations of the previous schemes, we propose a secure and fast query approach for high-precision multi-dimensional satellite remote sensing data, namely SFQA. In our scheme, we first construct an R-tree that covers all the high-precision multi-dimensional satellite remote sensing data and applies 0–1 encoding 18 and Bloom filter 19 techniques to process the minimum bounding rectangle (MBR) corresponding to each node in the R-tree. A secure and efficient encryption algorithm is then used to encrypt all the high-precision multi-dimensional satellite remote sensing data within the MBR. For ease of explanation, we refer to the described index as the secure R-tree index. We conduct extensive experiments to demonstrate the correctness and security of the proposed method.

We summarize our proposed scheme SFQA in the following three main aspects.

(1) We construct a secure R-tree index by using a normal R-tree, 0–1 encoding technique and Bloom filter.
(2) We propose a Secure and Fast Query Approach for High-precision Multi-dimensional Satellite Remote Sensing Data, namely SFQA, by using the proposed secure R-tree index.
(3) We conduct a large number of experiments to evaluate the efficiency and provide a thorough analysis of the security of the proposed approach SFQA.

The remaining sections of this paper are structured as follows. Section 2 provides an overview of related research. Section 3 introduces the essential preliminary knowledge. Section 4 outlines the system model. Section 5 presents the construction of our proposed scheme. Section 6 presents the experimental evaluation. Section 7 provides a detailed analysis of the security of our proposed scheme. Finally, Sect. 8 concludes this paper.

2 Related Work

There are mainly three classes of secure and fast query schemes for high-precision multi-dimensional satellite remote sensing data: order-preserving encryption schemes, bucketization schemes, and secure index schemes.

2.1 Order Preserving Encryption Schemes

Agrawal et al. 8 first proposed an Order-Preserving Encryption (OPE) scheme. Subsequently, Boldyreva et al. 20 proved that no OPE scheme can satisfy a rigorous security definition. Since then, many researchers have conducted extensive related studies based on the work of Boldyreva et al.20. However, most of these studies only consider OPE schemes for single-dimensional data and ignore the fact that there is a large amount of multi-dimensional data in the real world. Recently, Zhan et al. 12 proposed an efficient multi-dimensional order-preserving encryption scheme, namely MDOPE. This scheme uses a network data structure to organize multi-dimensional data and utilizes prefix encoding and Bloom filter techniques to process the values stored in the network data structure, making it possible to perform queries on encrypted multi-dimensional data.

2.2 Bucketization Schemes

In the bucketization scheme, data are grouped into different buckets. All the data in the same bucket are considered as a whole. When a query matches a bucket, all the data within that bucket are retrieved. The first bucketization scheme was proposed in 21. Subsequently, researchers analyzed how bucketization can improve both query security and efficiency 15. In subsequent work, Lee 22 proposed an ordered bucketization scheme to improve search efficiency. In Lee's scheme, all the buckets are organized in a certain order, i.e., all the data in one bucket is smaller than all the data in another bucket.

2.3 Secure Index Schemes

Peng Wang et al. 14 use asymmetric scalar-product preserving encryption (ASPE) 23 to process the buckets and construct a secure index called $\hat{R}$-tree. Mei et al. 17 also developed a secure bucket-based n-ary tree (each internal tree node links to n child nodes) index to support range queries over the ciphertexts of multi-dimensional data. However, the scheme 17 works well only for uniformly distributed datasets.

3 Preliminaries

In this section, we provide a brief overview of several key concepts central to our presentation, including R-tree 24, 0–1 encoding technique 25, and Bloom filter 19.

3.1 R-tree

The R-tree 24 is a height-balanced tree that can be used as an index structure for multi-dimensional data. Each node of the R-tree contains a minimum bounding rectangle (MBR). The MBR of an internal node covers the union of the MBRs of its child nodes. Each leaf node is linked to a bucket, and all the data covered by its MBR is stored in that bucket.

3.2 Bloom Filter

A Bloom filter 19 is a probabilistic data structure used to test whether an element is a member of a set. It consists of three parts, including (i) a bit array A of n bits, (ii) k independent hash functions $h_1, h_2, \ldots, h_k$, where $h_i : \{0, 1\}^* \rightarrow [1, n]$ and $i \in [1, k]$, , and (iii) a dataset $D = \{d_1, d_2, \ldots, d_m\}$ that contains m different data. Given data d', the Bloom filter can judge whether $d' \in D$ or $d' \notin D$ by using the following method.

(1) The Bloom filter initializes all the bits of the bit array A to 0.
(2) To add an element d_j to the Bloom filter, the filter calculates the hash value $h_i(d_j)$ and sets the bit at position $h_i(d_j)$ in the bit array A to 1, where $i \in [1, k]$ and $j \in [1, m]$.
(3) To test whether an element d' is in the dataset D, the Bloom filter calculates the hash value $h_i(d')$ for each of the k independent hash functions, where $i \in [1, k]$. If the bit at position $h_i(d')$ in the bit array A is 1, the data d' is considered to be a member of the dataset D. However, if any of the bits at these positions are 0, then d' is definitely not in D.

3.3 0–1 Encoding Technique

Let $s = s_n s_{n-1} \ldots s_1 \in {0, 1}^n$ be a binary string of length n. Its 0-encoding form is defined as a set $S_s^0 = \{s_n s_{n-1} \ldots s_{i+1} 1 | s_i = 0, 1 \le i \le n\}$. Similarly, its 1-encoding form is defined as a set $S_s^1 = \{s_n s_{n-1} \ldots s_i | s_i = 1, 1 \le i \le n\}$. Given two integers x and y, their 0–1 encoding forms can be used to judge whether $x > y$ or $x \le y$ as follows. Let S_x^0 be the 0-encoding form of x, S_x^1 be the 1-encoding form of x, S_y^0 be the 0-encoding form of y, and S_y^1 be the 1-encoding form of y. If and only if $S_x^1 \cap S_y^0 \neq \emptyset$, there is $x > y$. On the contrary, if and only if $S_x^1 \cap S_y^0 = \emptyset$, there is $x \le y$. The work 25 has proved the above conclusions clearly. We give an example to illustrate data comparison by 0–1 encoding forms. Given two data 11 and 6, the 4-bit binary strings are $(1011)_2$ and $(0110)_2$ respectively. It is easy to calculate the 0–1 encoding forms of 11 and 6, i.e., $S_{11}^1 = \{11\}$, $S_{11}^1 = \{1, 101, 1011\}$, $S_6^0 = \{1, 0111\}$ and $S_6^1 = \{01, 011\}$. As $S_{11}^1 \cap S_6^0 = \{1\} \neq \emptyset$, there is $11 > 6$. On the contrary, as $S_6^1 \cap S_{11}^0 = \emptyset$, there is $6 \le 11$.

4 System Model

The system model is shown in Fig. 1, which includes four entities: remote sensing data sources, semi-trusted data centers, data requesters, and trusted servers. The trusted server collects sensitive remote sensing data, builds a secure R-tree index, and encrypts it. Next, the trusted server uploads the secure R-tree index and the ciphertext to the semi-trusted

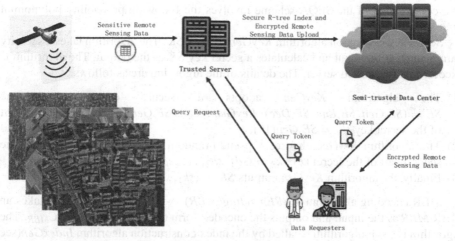

Fig. 1. System model.

data center. Data requesters send query requests to the trusted server and receive query tokens. Then, data requesters send the query tokens to the semi-trusted data center. Upon receiving the query tokens, the data center performs queries on the secure R-tree index and returns the query results. Finally, data requesters decrypt the ciphertext in the query results.

Definition 1: Security [12, 26]. Given a leakage function F, all adversaries A are unable to reveal more information than the leakage function F, then the scheme SFQA is considered secure. The leakage function is defined as $F(x, y) = position_{diff}(x, y)$, where $position_{diff}(x, y)$ returns the position of the first difference between x and y.

5   Construction of SFQA

This section first provides an overview of the construction process of our scheme SFQA. Then, we describe in detail the key generation algorithm, MBR encoding algorithm, index construction algorithm, query token generation algorithm, and range query algorithm. The scheme starts with the trusted server building a normal R-tree index over all the collected high-resolution multi-dimensional satellite remote sensing data. Each minimum bounding rectangle (MBR) in the normal R-tree index is then processed using the 0-encoding technique and Bloom filter, and encrypted. This way, the trusted server obtains a secure R-tree index and all the ciphertexts. Next, the trusted server outsources the secure R-tree index and the ciphertexts to the semi-trusted data center (a third-party server). Before performing a range query, a data requester sends the queried range to the trusted server. The trusted server generates several hash values as the query token using its secret key and hash functions in the Bloom filter and sends the query token to the data requester. Then, the data requester sends the query token to the semi-trusted data center. Upon receiving the query token, the semi-trusted data center performs a range query over the secure R-tree index in a top-down manner and returns the query results to the data requester. Finally, the data requester decrypts all the ciphertexts in the query results.

The construction of the SFQA scheme involves the following probability polynomial time algorithms.

Secret key generation algorithm $KeyGen(1^\lambda) \rightarrow SK$: The algorithm takes a security parameter λ as the input and calculates a secret key SK as the output. The algorithm is executed by the trusted server. The details of the algorithm are as follows.

(1) The algorithm $KeyGen$ adopts a secure encryption scheme $SE = (SE.Gen, SE.Enc, SE.Dec)$. $KeyGen$ recalls $SE.Gen$ to generate the first part of the secret key $sk_1 = SE.Gen(1^\lambda)$.
(2) The algorithm $KeyGen$ chooses k pseudo-random seeds $sd_1, sd_2, \ldots, sd_k$ as the second part of the secret key $sk_2 = (sd_1, sd_2, \ldots, sd_k)$.
(3) Finally, the algorithm $KeyGen$ outputs $SK = (sk_1, sk_2)$ as the secret key.

MBR encoding algorithm $MBREncoding(MBR) \rightarrow C_{MBR}$: The algorithm takes an MBR MBR as the input, and outputs the encoded form of MBR, denoted by C_{MBR}. The algorithm is a sub-algorithm recalled by the index construction algorithm $IndexGen$(see the following paragraphs). The details of the sub-algorithm are as follows.

For illustration purposes, we suppose $MBR = [a_1, b_1] \times [a_2, b_2] \times \ldots \times [a_d, b_d]$, where $[a_i, b_i]$ is the range on the i-th dimension, d is the dimensionality. The algorithm $MBREncoding$ encodes a_i to its binary string form, denoted by c_{a_i}, The length of a_i is set to l. For security concerns, the algorithm $MBREncoding$ randomizes the binary string forms of c_{a_i}. Namely, the algorithm $MBREncoding$ pads a l-length random binary string r_{a_i} after c_{a_i}, i.e., $c_{a_i}||r_{a_i}$. For data comparison purposes, the algorithm $MBREncoding$ calculates the 0-encoding form of $c_{a_i}||r_{a_i}$, denoted by $S^0_{c_{a_i}||r_{a_i}}$. By executing the same processes, the algorithm $MBREncoding$ calculates $S^0_{c_{b_i}||r_{b_i}}$. Then, uses the hash functions $h_1, h_2, \ldots, h_k$ in the Bloom filter and the second part secret key $sk_2 = (sd_1, sd_2, \ldots, sd_k)$ to process the binary strings in $S^0_{c_{a_i}||r_{a_i}}$ and $S^0_{c_{b_i}||r_{b_i}}$. Specifically, the sub-algorithm $MBREncoding$ calculates sets of hash values $V_{a_i} = \{h_1(s, sd_1), h_2(s, sd_2), \ldots, h_k(s, sd_k)|s \in S^0_{c_{a_i}||r_{a_i}}\}$ and $V_{b_i} = \{h_1(s, sd_1), h_2(s, sd_2), \ldots, h_k(s, sd_k)|s \in S^0_{c_{b_i}||r_{b_i}}\}$. Finally, the sub-algorithm $MBREncoding$ calculates the encoded form of MBR and outputs $C_{MBR} = \{< A_{a_i}, A_{b_i} > |i \in [1, d]\}$.

Example 1. As shown in Fig. 2, Through the algorithm $MBREncoding$, we can calculate the encoded form of $R = [a_1, b_1] \times [a_2, b_2]$, which is $C_R = \{< A_{a_1}, A_{b_1} >, < A_{a_2}, A_{b_2} >\}$.

Index construction algorithm $IndexGen(T) \rightarrow T^*$: The algorithm takes a normal R-tree T as the input and constructs a secure R-tree index T^* as the output. The details of the algorithm are as follows. First, the algorithm $IndexGen$ recalls the sub-algorithm $MBREncoding$ to process all the MBRs of nodes in the normal R-tree T. Then, the algorithm $IndexGen$ recalls the algorithm $SE.Enc$ to encrypt all the collected high-precision multi-dimensional satellite remote sensing data in groups which are under the leaf nodes of T. Finally, the algorithm $IndexGen$ outputs the secure R-tree index T^*.

The following Example 2 shows the generation of a secure R-tree index.

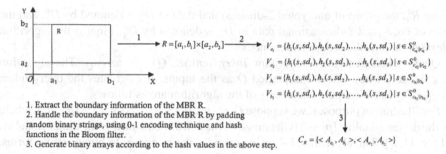

1. Extract the boundary information of the MBR R.
2. Handle the boundary information of the MBR R by padding
random binary strings, using 0-1 encoding technique and hash
functions in the Bloom filter.
3. Generate binary arrays according to the hash values in the above step.

$$C_R = \{< A_{a_1}, A_{b_1} >, < A_{a_2}, A_{b_2} >\}$$

Fig. 2. MBR Encoding.

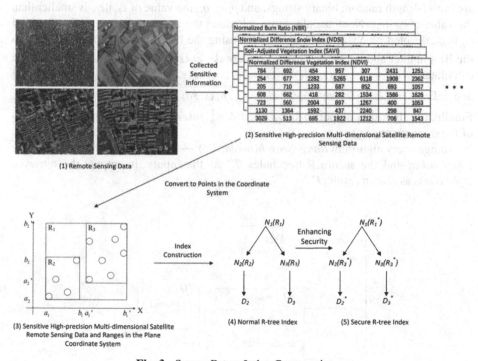

(1) Remote Sensing Data

(2) Sensitive High-precision Multi-dimensional Satellite Remote Sensing Data

(3) Sensitive High-precision Multi-dimensional Satellite Remote Sensing Data and Ranges in the Plane Coordinate System

(4) Normal R-tree Index

(5) Secure R-tree Index

Fig. 3. Secure R-tree Index Construction.

Example 2. As shown in Fig. 3 (1), high-precision multi-dimensional satellite remote sensing data are retrieved from satellites. Then, as shown in Fig. 3 (2), all the sensitive multi-dimensional satellite remote sensing data is stored in some tables. Next, as shown in Fig. 3 (3), all the sensitive multi-dimensional satellite remote sensing data is 2-dimensional and distributed in the planar coordinate system, which is represented by hollow circles. First, as shown in Fig. 3 (4), the trusted server builds a normal R-tree index over these 2-dimensional data. Then, the trusted server runs the algorithm *IndexGen*. The algorithm *IndexGen* recalls the sub-algorithm *MBREncoding* to process the MBRs R_1, R_2 and R_3, and recalls the algorithm *SE.Enc* to encrypt all the 2-dimensional data in D_2 and D_3 respectively. As shown in Fig. 3 (5), the processed MBRs are denoted by R_1^*,

R_2^* and R_3^*, the group of encrypted 2-dimensional data in D_2 is denoted by D_2^*, and the group of encrypted 2-dimensional data in D_3 is denoted by D_3^*. Finally, the algorithm *IndexGen* outputs the secure R-tree index.

Query token generation algorithm $TokenGen(SK, Q) \rightarrow token_Q$: The algorithm takes the secret key SK and a queried Q as the inputs. It calculates the query token $token_Q$ of Q as the output. The details of the algorithm are as follows.

For illustration purposes, we suppose $Q = [p_1, q_1] \times [p_2, q_2] \times \ldots \times [p_d, q_d]$, where d is the dimensionality, $[p_i, q_i]$ is the range on the i-th dimension, d is the dimensionality, and $i \in [1, d]$. The algorithm *TokenGen* encodes the p_i and q_i to binary string forms, denoted by c_{p_i} and c_{q_i}, then pads l-length random binary strings r_{p_i} and r_{q_i} after c_{p_i} and c_{q_i}. Specifically, the algorithm converts p_i and q_i to $c_{p_i}||r_{p_i}$ and $c_{q_i}||r_{q_i}$. As r_{p_i} and r_{q_i} are both l-length random binary strings, and $p_i < q_i$, the value of $c_{p_i}||r_{p_i}$ is smaller than the value of $c_{q_i}||r_{q_i}$. Next, the algorithm calculates the 1-encoding forms of $c_{p_i}||r_{p_i}$ and $c_{q_i}||r_{q_i}$, denoted by $S_{c_{p_i}||r_{p_i}}^1$ and $S_{c_{q_i}||r_{q_i}}^1$. By using the hash functions $h_1, h_2, \ldots, h_k$ in the Bloom filter and the second part secret key $sk_2 = (sd_1, sd_2, \ldots, sd_k)$, the algorithm calculates $token_p^1 = \{< h_1(s, sd_1), h_2(s, sd_2), \ldots, h_k(s, sd_k) > |s \in S_{c_{p_i}||r_{p_i}}^1, i \in [1, d]\}$ and $token_q^1 = \{< h_1(s, sd_1), h_2(s, sd_2), \ldots, h_k(s, sd_k) > |s \in S_{c_{q_i}||r_{q_i}}^1, i \in [1, d]\}$. Finally, the algorithm outputs $token_Q =< token_p^1, token_q^1 >$ as the query token $token_Q$ of the queried range Q.

Range query algorithm $RangeSearch(token, T^*) \rightarrow I^*$: The algorithm takes a query token *token* and the secure R-tree index T^* as the inputs. It outputs the retrieved ciphertexts as search results I^*.

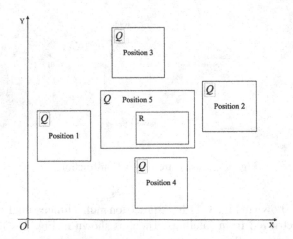

The minimal coordinate value in R is (a_1, a_2) The minimal coordinate value in R is (p_1, p_2)

The maximal coordinate value in R is (b_1, b_2) The maximal coordinate value in R is (q_1, q_2)

Fig. 4. The Judgment of Queried Range and MBR.

Firstly, we introduce how to judge whether a queried range Q intersects with an MBR MBR. Then, we introduce how to perform a range query over the secure R-tree index T^*.

As shown in Fig. 4, the queried range is $Q = [p_1, q_1] \times [p_2, q_2]$ and the MBR is $R = [a_1, b_1] \times [a_2, b_2]$. When R is at position 1, as $q_1 < a_1$ (according to the 0–1 encoding technique, $q_1 < a_1$ indicates $S^1_{c_{q_1} \| r_{q_1}} \cap S^0_{c_{a_1} \| r_{a_1}} = \emptyset$), there is $[p_1, q_1] \cap [a_1, b_1] = \emptyset$, i.e., $Q \cap R = \emptyset$. Thus, if $S^1_{c_{q_1} \| r_{q_1}} \cap S^0_{c_{a_1} \| r_{a_1}} = \emptyset$, there is $Q \cap R = \emptyset$. Similarly, when R is at position 2, position 3, position 4, and position 5, by using the above method, the algorithm *RangeSearch* can judge whether $Q \cap R \neq \emptyset$ and $R \subseteq Q$.

For ease of explanation, we suppose is a node in the secure R-tree index and N is associated with the MBR MBR. If the algorithm *RangeSearch* determines $MBR \subseteq Q$, the algorithm adds all the encrypted high-precision multi-dimensional satellite remote sensing data in MBR to the result set. If the algorithm *RangeSearch* determines $MBR \not\subseteq Q$ and $Q \cap MBR \neq \emptyset$, the algorithm continues to judge the MBRs of descendant nodes of N iteratively. When Q intersects with or covers the MBR of a leaf node, the algorithm adds all the encrypted high-precision multi-dimensional satellite remote sensing data in the MBR of the leaf node to the result set. By using the query token $token_Q = <$ $token^1_p, token^1_q >$, the algorithm *RangeSearch* performs range query in the secure R-tree index T^* in a top-down manner. Finally, the algorithm *RangeSearch* returns the search results I^* (i.e., result set) to the data requester as a response.

Decryption algorithm $Dec(SK, I^*) \rightarrow I$: The algorithm takes the retrieved ciphertexts I^* as the inputs. It outputs the plaintext I through decrypting the ciphertexts with the first part secret key sk_1, i.e. $I = SE.Dec(I^*, sk_1)$.

6 Experiments

In the experiments, we compare the $\hat{R} - tree$ scheme 14, the MDOPE scheme 12, and our scheme SFQA. These schemes are implemented on a personal computer with AMD Ryzen 5 2500U CPU and 8G Random Access Memory (RAM) by using Java language. In the $\hat{R} - tree$ scheme and the SFQA scheme, the fan-out of the indexes is set to 6. It means that each 2-dimensional range is divided into at most 6 smaller 2-dimensional ranges. To achieve fairness in experimental comparisons, in the MDOPE scheme, each node on the 1st dimension contains only 1 split data, and each node on the 2nd dimension contains 2 split data. This is because the range on the 1st dimension is divided into 2 smaller ranges by using 1 split data, and the range on the 2nd dimension is divided into 3 smaller ranges by using 2 split data. According to the Cartesian product, in the MDOPE scheme, a 2-dimensional range is divided into 6 smaller 2-dimensional ranges. Additionally, MDOPE supports accurate range queries. To compare the MDOPE scheme, the $\hat{R} - tree$ scheme, and the SFQA scheme fairly, we set the MBR of each leaf node in the $\hat{R} - tree$ scheme and the SFQA scheme only contains 1 data.

In our experiments, we choose the remote sensing imagery of the surrounding area of New York City and extract its high-precision multi-dimensional satellite remote sensing data to test the efficiency of the above schemes. The remote sensing imagery of the surrounding area of New York City is shown in Fig. 5 and the high-precision multi-dimensional satellite remote sensing data of its Normalized Difference Vegetation Index

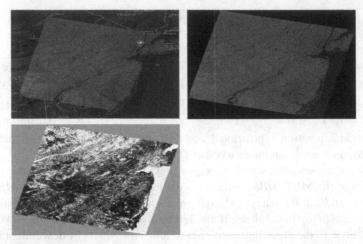

Fig. 5. Remote sensing imagery of the surrounding area of New York City.

(NDVI) is as shown in Fig. 6. We extract the high-precision multi-dimensional satellite remote sensing data of its NDVI as the tested high-precision 2-dimensional satellite remote sensing data.

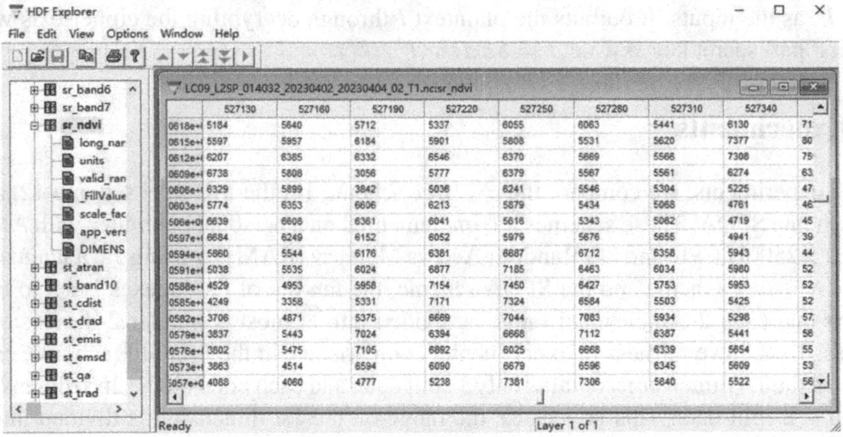

	527130	527160	527190	527220	527250	527280	527310	527340	
0618e+(	5184	5640	5712	5337	6055	6063	5441	6130	71
0615e+(	5597	5957	6184	5901	5808	5531	5620	7377	80
0612e+(	6207	6385	6332	6546	6370	5669	5566	7308	75
0609e+(	6738	5808	3056	5777	6379	5567	5561	6274	63
0606e+(	6329	5899	3842	5036	6241	5546	5304	5225	47
0603e+(	5774	6353	6606	6213	5879	5434	5068	4761	46
506e+0(	6639	6608	6361	6041	5616	5343	5062	4719	45
0597e+(	6684	6249	6152	6052	5979	5676	5655	4941	39
0594e+(	5860	5544	6176	6381	6687	6712	6358	5943	44
0591e+(	5038	5535	6024	6877	7185	6463	6034	5980	52
0588e+(	4529	4953	5958	7154	7450	6427	5753	5953	52
0585e+(	4249	3358	5331	7171	7324	6584	5503	5425	52
0582e+(	3706	4871	5375	6669	7044	7083	5934	5298	57
0579e+(	3837	5443	7024	6394	6668	7112	6387	5441	58
0576e+(	3802	5475	7105	6892	6025	6668	6339	5654	55
0573e+(	3863	4514	6594	6090	6679	6596	6345	5609	53
5057e+0	4088	4060	4777	5238	7381	7306	5840	5522	56

Fig. 6. Remote sensing data of the surrounding area of New York City.

Range Query. As shown in Fig. 7 (a), when the number of remote sensing data is fixed at 10000 and the length of the bit string increases, the search time is almost unchanged. As shown in Fig. 7 (b), when the number of remote sensing data increases, the search times of the SFQA scheme, the $\hat{R}-tree$ scheme, and the MDOPE scheme increase. Compared with the $\hat{R}-tree$ scheme and the MDOPE scheme, the SFQA scheme is the most efficient.

As shown in Fig. 7 (a), the search time of the $\hat{R}-tree$ scheme is almost unchanged because the length of the bit string does not relate to the underlying encryption method

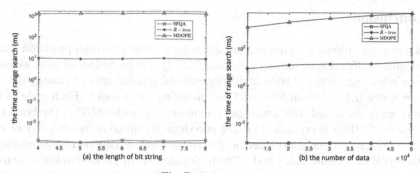

Fig. 7. Range Query.

ASPE. In the SFQA scheme and the MDOPE scheme, when the length of the bit string increases, the additional calculation overhead is very low, which results in the search times almost not increasing. As shown in Fig. 7 (b), when the number of remote sensing data increases, the heights of the indexes increase, which results in the $\hat{R} - tree$ scheme, the MDOPE scheme, and the SFQA scheme doing more range query works over these indexes. Thus, the search times of these schemes increase with the number of remote sensing data. In the MDOPE scheme, many split data are inserted into the internal nodes of the index to support range queries. Many comparison works over split data result in the low efficiency of range query. Additionally, the range query should be performed alone in each dimension respectively. Thus, the range query in the MDOPE scheme is not very efficient. As the underlying hash value comparison in the SFQA scheme is more efficient than the ASPE scheme in the $\hat{R} - tree$ scheme, the SFQA scheme is more efficient than the $\hat{R} - tree$ scheme.

7 Security Analysis

Theorem 1. The SFQA scheme satisfies the security property defined in Definition 1.

Proof 1. Since the data is encrypted using a secure encryption method, the security of the data can be ensured by the encryption method.

In the SFQA scheme, the data are encrypted by using a secure encryption scheme SE. The security of MBRs in the secure R-tree index can be analyzed in the following ways. The MBRs are processed by using the padding, the 0–1 encoding, and the Bloom filter. The security of the data can be guaranteed by the security of the secure encryption scheme SE. Suppose that (i) $x = x_1x_2 \ldots x_n$ represents the boundary information of an MBR after being padded with a random value (as described in Sect. 5), and (ii) $y = y_1y_2 \ldots y_n$ represents the boundary information of a queried range after being padded with a random value (as described in Sect. 5). If the member in the intersection of $S^0_{c_x\|r_x}$ and $S^1_{c_y\|r_y}$ is t, where the length of t is m, it can deduce that $x_1 = y_1, x_2 = y_2,$ $\ldots, x_{m-1} = y_{m-1}, x_m \neq y_m$. As a result, the semi-trusted data center is only aware of the leakage function $F(x, y) = position_{diff}(x, y)$. Thus, the SFQA scheme satisfies the security property defined in Definition 1.

8 Conclusion

In this paper, we propose a secure and fast querying approach for high-precision multi-dimensional satellite remote sensing data, namely SFQA. In the SFQA scheme, we build a secure index over high-precision multi-dimensional satellite remote sensing data by using an R-tree index, Bloom filter, and 0–1 encoding technologies. Each node of the secure index is associated with a minimum bounding rectangle (MBR). The boundary information of MBRs is processed by 0–1 encoding. By utilizing the property of 0–1 encoding, the semi-trusted data center can determine whether a queried range intersects with the MBR of a secure index node. The hash functions in the Bloom filter are used to ensure the security of the queried range and the MBRs of the secure index nodes. Thus, the proposed SFQA scheme can support secure and efficient range queries over high-precision multi-dimensional satellite remote sensing data.

Acknowledgement. This research is supported by the National Natural Science Foundation of China (No. 61962029, No. 62062045, No. 62262033), the Jiangxi Provincial Natural Science Foundation of China (No. 20202BAB212006), and the Science and Technology Research Project of Jiangxi Education Department (No. GJJ201832).

References

1. Boulila, W., Khlifi, M.K., Ammar, A., Koubaa, A., Benjdira, B., Farah, I.R.: A hybrid privacy-preserving deep learning approach for object classification in very high-resolution satellite images. Remote Sensing **14**, 4631 (2022)
2. Zhang, B., et al.: Progress and challenges in intelligent remote sensing satellite systems. IEEE J. Selected Topics Appl. Earth Observ. Remote Sens. **15**, 1814–1822 (2022)
3. Zhang, X., Zhang, G., Huang, X., Poslad, S.: Granular content distribution for IoT remote sensing data supporting privacy preservation. Remote Sensing **14**, 5574 (2022)
4. Wang, Z., Ma, Y., Zhang, Y., Shang, J.: Review of remote sensing applications in grassland monitoring. Remote Sensing **14**, 2903 (2022)
5. Michler, J.D., Josephson, A., Kilic, T., Murray, S.: Privacy protection, measurement error, and the integration of remote sensing and socioeconomic survey data. J. Dev. Econ. **158**, 102927 (2022)
6. Zhang, D.; Shafiq, M.; Wang, L.; Srivastava, G.; Yin, S.: Privacy-preserving remote sensing images recognition based on limited visual cryptography. CAAI Transactions on Intelligence Technology 8(4) (2023)
7. Nduku, L., et al.: Global research trends for unmanned aerial vehicle remote sensing application in wheat crop monitoring. Geomatics **3**, 115–136 (2023)
8. Agrawal, R.; Kiernan, J.; Srikant, R.; Xu, Y. Order preserving encryption for numeric data. In: Proceedings of the Proceedings of the 2004 ACM SIGMOD International Conference on Management of Data, 2004, pp. 563–574 (2004)
9. Peng, Y., Li, H., Cui, J., Zhang, J., Ma, J., Peng, C.: HOPE: improved order preserving encryption with the power to homomorphic operations of ciphertexts. SCIENCE CHINA Inf. Sci. **60**(6), 1–17 (2017). https://doi.org/10.1007/s11432-016-0242-7
10. Popa, R.A.; Redfield, C.M.; Zeldovich, N.; Balakrishnan, H. CryptDB: Protecting confidentiality with encrypted query processing. In: Proceedings of the Proceedings of the Twenty-Third ACM Symposium on Operating Systems Principles, pp. 85–100 (2011)

11. Quan, H., Wang, B., Zhang, Y., Wu, G.: Efficient and secure top-k queries with top order-preserving encryption. IEEE Access **6**, 31525–31540 (2018)
12. Zhan, Y., Shen, D., Duan, P., Zhang, B., Hong, Z., Wang, B.: MDOPE: efficient multi-dimensional data order preserving encryption scheme. Inf. Sci. **595**, 334–343 (2022)
13. David, H.A.; Nagaraja, H.N. Order statistics; John Wiley & Sons (2004)
14. Wang, P., Ravishankar, C.V.: Secure and efficient range queries on outsourced databases using Rp-trees. In: Proceedings of the 594 2013 IEEE 29th International Conference on Data Engineering (ICDE). IEEE, 2013, pp. 314–325 (2013)
15. Hore, B., Mehrotra, S., Tsudik, G.: A privacy-preserving index for range queries. In: Proceedings of the Proceedings of the Thirtieth International Conference on Very Large Data Bases-Volume 30, 2004, pp. 720–731. (2004)
16. Hore, B., Mehrotra, S., Canim, M., Kantarcioglu, M.: Secure multidimensional range queries over outsourced data. VLDB J. **21**, 333–358 (2012)
17. Mei, Z., et al.: Executing multi-dimensional range query efficiently and flexibly over outsourced ciphertexts in the cloud. Inf. Sci. **432**, 79–96 (2018)
18. Gupta, P., McKeown, N.: Algorithms for packet classification. IEEE Network **15**, 24–32 (2001)
19. Bloom, B.H.: Space/time trade-offs in hash coding with allowable errors. Commun. ACM **13**, 422–426 (1970)
20. Boldyreva, A., Chenette, N., Lee, Y., O'Neill, A.: Order-preserving symmetric encryption. In: Joux, A. (ed.) Advances in Cryptology - EUROCRYPT 2009, pp. 224–241. Springer Berlin Heidelberg, Berlin, Heidelberg (2009). https://doi.org/10.1007/978-3-642-01001-9_13
21. Hacigümüş, H., Iyer, B., Li, C., Mehrotra, S.: Executing SQL over encrypted data in the database-service-provider model. In: Proceedings of the Proceedings of the 2002 ACM SIGMOD International Conference on Management of Data, 2002, pp. 216–227 (2002)
22. Lee, Y.: Secure ordered bucketization. IEEE Trans. Dependable Secure Comput. **11**, 292–303 (2014)
23. Wong, W.K., Cheung, D.W.l., Kao, B.; Mamoulis, N.: Secure kNN computation on encrypted databases. In: Proceedings of the Proceedings of the 2009 ACM SIGMOD International Conference on Management of data, 2009, pp. 139–152 (2009)
24. Guttman, A. R-trees: a dynamic index structure for spatial searching. In: Proceedings of the Proceedings of the 1984 ACM SIGMOD International Conference on Management of Data, 1984, pp. 47–57 (1984)
25. Lin, H.-Y., Tzeng, W.-G.: An efficient solution to the millionaires' problem based on homomorphic encryption. In: Ioannidis, J., Keromytis, A., Yung, M. (eds.) ACNS 2005. LNCS, vol. 3531, pp. 456–466. Springer, Heidelberg (2005). https://doi.org/10.1007/11496137_31
26. Guo, J., Wang, J., Zhang, Z., Chen, X.: An almost non-interactive order preserving encryption scheme. In: Chunhua, Su., Kikuchi, H. (eds.) Information Security Practice and Experience: 14th International Conference, ISPEC 2018, Tokyo, Japan, September 25-27, 2018, Proceedings, pp. 87–100. Springer International Publishing, Cham (2018). https://doi.org/10.1007/978-3-319-99807-7_6

Data Operation and Management Practices in Ping an Group

Zhang Sensen[1], Wei Kai[2], and Jiang Xin[3]([envelope])

[1] Ping An Technology (Shenzhen) Co., Ltd., Nanjing 210000, China
[2] Ping An Technology (Shenzhen) Co., Ltd., Shenzhen 518054, China
[3] Ping An Technology (Shenzhen) Co., Ltd., Beijing 100000, China
JIANGXIN502@pingan.com.cn

Abstract. In the context of the rapid development of information technology and the era of big data, data has transformed into a key asset for enterprises. As one of China's largest comprehensive financial service providers, Ping An Group has been committed to promoting data compliance management and the protection of personal information. The group has built a comprehensive data management system to ensure the compliant use of data while helping the business develop efficiently. This article introduces in detail Ping An Group's "one system + four mechanisms" data management and operation system. It also focuses on the main practices and important results achieved in the group's data compliance operations, personal information protection, and data interaction management. The experience shows how to achieve efficient data flow and maximize corporate benefits while complying with laws and regulations, providing valuable reference for other financial and quasi-financial companies.

Keywords: Data management · Data compliance · Personal information protection

1 Important Challenges Faced by Ping An Group's Data Management and Operations

With the successive introduction of a series of laws and regulations such as the "Personal Information Protection Law" and the "Data Security Law," national and industry regulatory authorities have imposed stricter requirements on enterprises for compliant data management and data security protection. As a leading group enterprise in the industry, Ping An Group regards safeguarding information security and ensuring data compliance as the bottom line that determines the survival or demise of the company. At the same time, Ping An has a strategic imperative to accelerate its digital transformation,

---

* Jiang Xin is the head of the data management team of the Security Center of Ping An Group's Science and Technology Association. He joined Ping An Group in 2020 and has been responsible for the Group's data management and personal information protection since 2021, and has promoted the construction of the Group's data compliance system, mechanism, and application system.

J. Feng et al. (Eds.): EDGE 2023, LNCS 14205, pp. 82–91, 2024.
https://doi.org/10.1007/978-3-031-51826-3_8

vigorously drive business innovation, and empower comprehensive financial services. Therefore, how to fully utilize data as a critical corporate asset, promote business revenue growth, and improve efficiency while ensuring compliance has become a crucial issue.

Ping An Group is a leading group enterprise in the industry with more than 30 member companies, each having differences in business forms, scales, management methods, and regulatory requirements. These differences make the aforementioned issues even more complex and challenging. In this complex context, how to strictly adhere to compliance, continuously safeguard customer privacy, maintain the brand image, and make full use of data to unleash its value are the core issues that concern our data management and operational work.

2 Data Management System of Ping An Group

Ping An Group's data management system is based on three core elements: compliance, management and technology. The main goal of this system is to ensure data compliance and improve data usage efficiency. In order to achieve this goal, Ping An Group designs and plans according to the framework of "one system + four mechanisms". The "one system" here refers to the group data management and monitoring system, while the "four mechanisms" include management mechanism, authorization mechanism, supervision mechanism and asset management mechanism.The four mechanisms are key to ensuring data compliance, and the monitoring system is crucial for implementing these compliance safeguard mechanisms.

First of all, the management mechanism involves the organizations, systems and processes related to various management tasks. Ping An Group has clarified the functions of data management and comprehensively promoted the implementation of data compliance by formulating a series of data management systems. At the same time, Ping An Group also actively promotes the standardization of data compliance management, promotes the improvement of data compliance system from the group level, and provides framework specifications and guidance for the construction of system systems of various member companies.

Secondly, the authorization mechanism mainly covers two aspects: data authorization network and personal information authorization information management. Ping An Group is guided by regulations, combined with internal data usage methods, and based on the "Great Wall Clauses" to promote the construction of relevant privacy agreements, data entrustment agreements, data sharing agreements and other agreement networks. At the same time, Ping An Group has built a two-level personal information authorized collection, management and authentication service system to ensure the compliant use of personal information.

Thirdly, the supervisory mechanism is a vital safeguard within Ping An Group's data management system. In order to ensure the effective implementation of various data management regulations and mechanisms, Ping An Group has established a tracking and review system and designed a method for evaluating data management capabilities, along with the initial development of a data management capability index system. Through various review activities conducted at the three stages of data usage - before, during, and after - a standardized assessment is carried out on the data management efforts of various organizational levels. This assessment helps evaluate and enhance the level of data management capabilities.

Finally, the asset management mechanism focuses on optimizing and improving the management standardization and usage efficiency of data assets. Based on data asset management tools, Ping An Group has supplemented and improved basic data information and provided technical support for the key data application and approval process. Through cooperation with the customer service department, Ping An Group has optimized its data compliance emergency incident handling mechanism and improved the efficiency and standardization of handling compliance incidents. In addition, Ping An Group has also optimized the shared data directory, data sharing compliance approval and other processes to promote the flow of data based on compliance.

Generally speaking, Ping An Group's data management system is based on compliance, uses management as a means, and uses technology as a guarantee. It comprehensively ensures data compliance and improves the efficiency of data resource use. Based on the above four major mechanisms, Ping An Group has sorted out three key data management tasks, including: data compliance operations, personal information protection and data interaction management.

3   Data Compliance Operations of Ping An Group

In addition to increasingly stringent legal regulations and regulatory requirements, there has been a growing awareness of privacy protection among users in recent years. Complaints related to the unauthorized collection and use of personal information within the industry have also become more frequent. Ping An Group, as a leading domestic large-scale financial holding company, has drawn the attention of regulatory authorities in the field of data compliance.

In this context, Ping An Group actively responds to policy directives and has constructed a data compliance operational framework known as the "Four Predictions" (Prediction, Prevention, Early Warning, and Pre-action). The creation of this framework not only encompasses comprehensive risk prediction, effective prevention, timely warnings, and appropriate pre-action, but more importantly, it finely manages the entire data process to ensure the legal and efficient use of data and fully tap into its potential value.

This system employs a "expert + tool" model, involving the stages of data ownership, data processing, and data utilization, and conducts a comprehensive review, collection, and analysis. It carries out relevant management activities through four major steps: risk assessment, work rectification, monitoring effectiveness, and emergency response. This approach comprehensively promotes and oversees the implementation of data compliance requirements and the enhancement of data management capabilities across all member companies. (see Fig. 1).

In the prediction process, Ping An Group uses risk profiling technology to comprehensively predict the risks that various member companies may encounter in aspects such as personal authorization, data processing, and data use, so as to ensure the pertinence of risk management. The risk assessment covers multiple dimensions such as personal privacy protection risks, key data management risks, data interaction violation

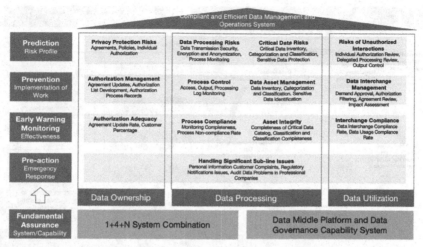

Fig. 1. "The Four Predictions" Data Operations System and Fundamental Institutional Capability Assurance

risks, illegal use of personal information risks, and data technology protection risks. The specific content includes evaluating the legality of the privacy agreement during the data collection stage and the key data list., data classification system, data entrustment processing agreement, data licensing and authorization, etc.

In the prevention process, Ping An Group formulated annual key tasks based on the risk profile analysis results, implemented them into the daily management of each member company, and conducted periodic monthly monitoring and semi-annual inspections. The main key tasks include determining the responsible person, clarifying the scope of key data, data classification and classification, personal authorization, data interaction management, data processing and use, and full-process data security management. The execution and monitoring of these tasks ensure that risk-related data work can be effectively implemented (see Fig. 2).

In the early warning phase, through a closed-loop management process involving monitoring, analysis, assessment, and targeted improvements, Ping An Group is able to promptly identify various data compliance risks. The monitoring indicator system encompasses five major categories, including institutional and system management, personal information authorization management, data asset management, data interchange and usage management, and comprehensive data processing management. It consists of over 60 detection and management indicators, with the primary goal of closely monitoring the progress and effectiveness of annual work.

In the pre-operation stage, Ping An Group has formulated detailed emergency plans for personal information use risk events and clarified team responsibilities and disposal procedures to ensure that personal information use risk events are effectively monitored and handled. On this basis, Ping An Group has established an emergency response organization composed of an incident decision-making group, an incident response group, and an incident handling group, each of which is responsible for its own responsibilities and jointly responds to personal information use risk events.

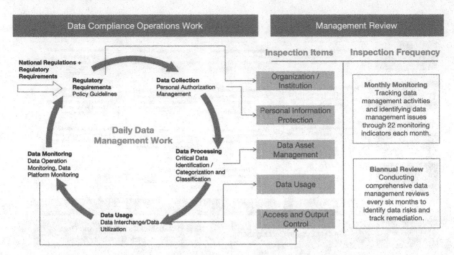

Fig. 2. Implementation and Review of Data Compliance Work

Ping An Group's data compliance operation system is built under multiple requirements such as national laws and regulations, superior regulatory authorities, national standards, and internal data security-related requirements of the enterprise. It covers the management of the entire data process and enables early prediction, prevention, early warning and pre-action of risks, thereby effectively ensuring data compliance and providing a solid guarantee for the steady development of the business. This successful practice of Ping An Group also provides a valuable reference and learning experience for the industry.

4   Personal Information Protection Strategy of Ping an Group

With the official implementation of the "Personal Information Protection Law" on November 1, 2021, various companies have updated the "privacy policies" of their Internet platform applications to meet new requirements such as personal information classification protection and automated decision-making rules proposed in the new law, undoubtedly it is the top priority right now [1]. However, as a basic law, the Personal Information Protection Law imposes new requirements on corporate personal information and data protection that go far beyond this. The "Personal Information Protection Law", the "Data Security Law" and the "Cybersecurity Law" go hand in hand, and together constitute the basic system of data protection compliance obligations that Chinese enterprises should abide by. Our focus should not be limited to a certain risk point, but should conduct a comprehensive review of our own business and products, and expand our perspective to the entire compliance system. Based on this, Ping An Group has conducted in-depth research, study and interpretation of major laws and regulations, formulated relevant mechanisms for personal information protection accordingly, and made every effort to promote the implementation of personal information protection work.

4.1 Key Responsibilities in Personal Information Data Management

As an important responsible entity for personal information protection, enterprises must carry out their personal information protection efforts systematically, routinely, and continuously. Personal information protection should be considered as one of the essential aspects of daily operational management, and it may even be elevated to the strategic level of the organization. This typically involves at least two critical areas of work: firstly, establishing a sound organizational structure include consider establishing an independent supervision agency composed of external members [2], and secondly, continually improving the data compliance management system.

4.2 Organizational Assurance for Personal Information Data Management

According to relevant regulatory requirements, when an enterprise employs more than 200 people and processes or is expected to process personal information of more than one million individuals or processes sensitive personal information of more than 100,000 individuals, it is mandatory to designate a person responsible for personal information protection. In practice, a full-time personal information protection officer should be established at the company level rather than at the department level. This responsible individual is involved in critical decisions related to personal information processing activities and reports directly to the company's top management. Considering cost control and the current stage of development of the organization, the personal information protection officer can also be a part-time role, for example, held by the Chief Data Officer (CDO), Chief Information Officer (CIO), or Chief Legal Counsel. In addition, the enterprise should establish a complete organizational structure for personal information protection. Based on our time-tested experience, a mature organizational structure can typically be built around the following framework (see Fig. 3):

4.3 Operational Mechanism for Personal Information Data Management

Based on the requirements of national laws and regulations, enterprises should establish a comprehensive "end-to-end data security management system." In terms of the construction of the personal information protection system, three key aspects are further clarified:

1. Establish and implement systems based on the five fundamental principles: the legal and legitimate collection principle, the minimal necessary principle, the openness and transparency principle, the data quality principle, and the data security principle.
2. Develop internal special compliance regulations and operational procedures based on the purpose of personal information processing, processing methods, types of personal information, potential impacts on individual rights, and possible security risks. These regulations should include, at a minimum, general guidelines for personal information protection, rules for personal information collection, rules for personal information use, rules for sensitive personal information processing, policies for personal information storage and retention, rules for personal information sharing, transfer, and entrusted processing, rules for cross-border personal information transfer, rules for

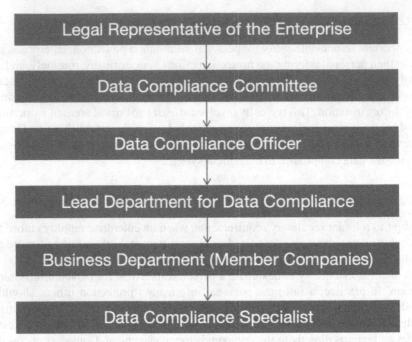

Fig. 3. Personal Information Protection Organizational Structure

personal information security incident handling, and rules for personal information disclosure.

3. Develop a personal information security incident emergency response plan, which should include the organization and working mechanism for security incident emergency response, responsibility mechanisms, how to record, assess, and report personal information security incidents, how to fulfill the obligation to inform the data subjects, and a training and drill plan for emergency response [3].

Therefore, companies should establish a hierarchical management mechanism for personal information in accordance with relevant regulatory requirements to protect different categories of personal information, especially sensitive personal information and information about minors [4].Companies should also establish a mechanism for publicizing personal information processing rules, clearly and comprehensively informing individuals about the company's personal information processing rules. Before conducting personal information processing activities with significant impacts, companies should conduct a preliminary assessment of the impact on personal information protection and document the processing details. Additionally, companies need to conduct periodic security audits of their compliance with personal information processing.

Both the organizational assurance and the mechanism construction of enterprises are not static. Enterprises must closely follow the regulatory supplementary provisions, regulatory enforcement criteria, judicial tendencies by relevant government departments, and establish a compliance-oriented perspective on personal information protection. Enterprises should also establish mechanisms for reporting and investigating violations of personal information protection, and assess the effectiveness of security training and education to prevent risks. These mechanisms provide safeguards for the effective implementation of personal information protection systems and operational mechanisms [5].

4.4 Main Practices in Protecting Personal Information in Ping An Group

In order to meet the relevant requirements of laws and regulations, resist related risks, and comply with compliance requirements, Ping An Group has adopted a series of coordinated measures to jointly promote the comprehensive implementation of data compliance management:

First of all, Ping An Group advocates the construction of agreement network, which is embodied in the extensive promotion of "Great Wall Clauses". On the premise of complying with national laws, regulations and regulatory requirements, the Group has taken a series of measures to ensure that the collection and use of users' personal information reaches compliance. For APP front-end authorization, the compliance department has provided a series of relevant terms, such as the "Privacy Policy", "User Agreement" and "Great Wall Terms", etc., to ensure that users are fully and completely guaranteed their right to know, and at the same time, they also obtain the user's right to know. Personal information authorization. For the collection and use of back-end data, the Data Management Department will promote it to each company based on the agreement text provided by the Compliance Department. The main agreements include the "Data Sharing Agreement" and the "Data Entrusted Processing Agreement", and the authorization is clearly stipulated in the agreement. Information fields, content and purpose.

Secondly, Ping An Group adopted the "Taishan Plan" to comprehensively optimize personal information authorization management specifications and capability management mechanisms, and also upgraded personal authorization records and authentication management mechanisms. The main work includes four aspects:

1. The text structuring processing capability of the authorization agreement converts the natural language of the text content into a structured digital expression that can be recognized and understood by the system, so as to effectively manage authorization information;
2. Record and retain authorization information, record, store and manage multiple pieces of authorization flow information generated by users' agreement selections in different channels, different businesses, and different touchpoint scenarios;
3. Query and use of authorization information, promote data processors to conduct effective and timely authorization queries when processing, sharing and using personal information, and carry out various data applications in compliance based on authentication results.
4. Authorization management assessment and evaluation, establish an effective evaluation and assessment mechanism guarantee, including establishing a mechanism to regularly verify the timeliness and accuracy of authorization information records, as well as a mechanism to standardize authorization inquiry and use, and establish compliant and efficient authorization inquiry capabilities, etc..

With the orderly advancement of personal information protection work within Ping An Group, the current coverage rate for personal information authorization has reached 100%, and the coverage rate for personal information usage authentication has also reached 100%. There have been zero personal information security incidents so far.

5 Data Interchange Management Practice in Ping An Group

Data Interchange Management refers to an organization establishing data interchange mechanisms, standardizing data interchange activities, and ensuring that data assets are interacted with internally in a compliant and efficient manner. This is crucial for breaking down data barriers across various member companies, accelerating the efficient flow of data assets within the group, maximizing their utility, and empowering business operations. Additionally, data interchange management must ensure data compliance and security, treating compliance with data regulations and personal information protection as fundamental "red lines."

To ensure the compliance of data interchange processes and support the efficient flow and usage of data, Ping An Group has established a standardized data interchange application and usage process. This process includes seven steps: feasibility communication, demand initiation, data asset enhancement, demand approval, data provisioning, demand processing, demand acceptance, and feedback. At the same time, the Group clearly defines the main participants in the process and outlines their responsibilities and obligations, primarily including data requestors, data providers, data processors, and the Group's security center (compliance management). Each party in the interchange application process bears its own responsibilities, collaborates to manage the project, and focuses on resolving disputed issues through discussion and negotiation, all while ensuring data interchange compliance and maximizing work efficiency (see Fig. 4).

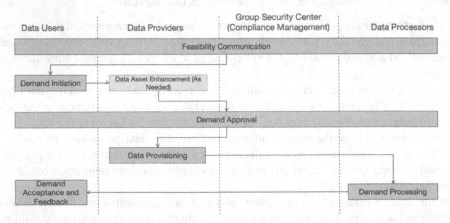

Fig. 4. Data Interchange Application and Approval Process

In terms of safeguard mechanisms, Ping An Group embeds compliance review and control measures at every stage of data collection and processing, including data access and output, data storage, data processing, data utilization, data deletion, interaction logs, and emergency response, to ensure the security and compliance of data. Additionally, for the inspection mechanism of data interchange, the Group's Security Center Data Management Team regularly supervises and inspects the execution of data interchange, identifying and improving issues. Moreover, all relevant parties involved in data interchange are required to conduct self-inspections regularly and promptly address any issues identified during the self-inspection.

Ping An Group's data interchange safeguard mechanism ensures the effective implementation in Group. While promoting the efficient flow of data, it firmly upholds compliance standards, achieving zero compliance risks, zero regulatory penalties, and zero customer complaints in practice.

6 Summarize

Ping An Group, guided by the principle of "Ensuring Compliance and Promoting Efficiency," has established a data management system with the framework of "One System, Four Mechanisms." Based on this framework, the Group has actively engaged in various important activities, including data compliance operations, personal information protection, and data interchange compliance. It has proactively advanced the practice of data operations and management, comprehensively elevating the Group's data compliance management capabilities and enabling efficient data resource circulation. This approach ensures that data is properly managed, used in compliance with regulations, and empowers business operations.

The Group's data management and operational efforts have achieved remarkable results, including 100% customer authorization coverage, 100% authentication for personal information usage,, zero compliance risks in practice, zero regulatory penalties, and zero customer privacy complaints. Looking ahead, Ping An Group will continue to prioritize data, continuously optimize data operations and management, and provide strong support for the Group's digital transformation journey.

References

1. Ximei, W., Fujia, D.: Interpretation of the personal information protection law in the era of big data. J. Jiaozuo Univ. **2**, 12–16 (2023)
2. Yue, S.: Enterprise data compliance and its construction in the era of digital economy. Hubei Soc. Sci. **8**, 119–128 (2022)
3. Qianshi, W.: Analysis of data compliance management path based on personal information protection. Cult. Educ. Mater. **6**, 192–195 (2022)
4. Weiqun, H.: Personal Information Protection based on Classification and Grading. Inf. Secur. Commun. Priv. **10**, 107–114 (2021)
5. Yixiao, M.: Research on data protection compliance system. J. National Prosecutor's Coll. **2**, 84–100 (2022)

Author Index

J. Feng et al. (Eds.): EDGE 2023, LNCS 14205, p. 93, 2024.
https://doi.org/10.1007/978-3-031-51826-3

Printed in the United States
by Baker & Taylor Publisher Services

Printed in the United States
by Baker & Taylor Publisher Services